Japane

Time

For my friend and brother, Barry Doyle, (1967–2008), who encouraged me to keep fighting and being.

Chris Robinson's books include *Estonian Animation: Between Genius and Utter Illiteracy* (2003 & 2006), *Unsung Heroes of Animation* (2005) and *Canadian Animation: Looking for a Place to Happen* (2008).

Japanese Animation: Time out of Mind

by Chris Robinson

British Library Cataloguing in Publication Data

Japanese Animation: Time out of Mind

A catalogue entry for this book is available from the British Library

ISBN: 9780 86196 692 9 (Paperback)

"Yesterday, today and tomorrow are all in the same room. There's no telling what can happen".
Billy the Kid (Richard Gere) in *I'm Not There*

"Aimai is defined as a state in which there is more than one intended meaning, resulting in obscurity, indistinctness and uncertainty. ... Ambiguity is indispensable for maintaining harmony in Japanese life."
Roger Davies, *The Japanese Mind*

Published by
John Libbey Publishing Ltd, 3 Leicester Road, New Barnet, Herts EN5 5EW, United Kingdom
e-mail: john.libbey@orange.fr; web site: www.johnlibbey.com
Direct orders (UK and Europe): direct.orders@marston.co.uk

Distributed in N. America by **Indiana University Press**, 601 North Morton St, Bloomington, IN 47404, USA. www.iupress.indiana.edu

Distributed in Australasia by **Elsevier Australia**, Elsevier Australia, Tower 1, 475 Victoria Ave, Chatswood NSW 2067, Australia. www.elsevier.com.au

Printed and bound in Malaysia by Vivar Printing Sdn. Bhd., 48000 Rawang, Selangor Darul Ehsan

The programme

Introduction

This book came about through guilt. In 2006, I was accepted into a unique visitor's program by the Japan Foundation. The program offered me an all-expenses paid trip to Japan for two weeks. They flew me in, put me up, provided me with an escort and a translator. I was then told that I could pretty much pick what I wanted to do and see during those two weeks.

I know. Pretty hard to believe.

Feeling somewhat guilty, I decided that I should make the most of the trip and write a book about Japanese animation. I approached John Libbey, who has published a few of my books, and he expressed immediate interest.

The trip to Japan finally happened in January 2007. I visited Tokyo, Hiroshima and, my favourite, Kyoto. Along the way, I saw many sites and met and interviewed various animators.

Unfortunately, the interviews didn't turn out so great. I was exhausted and sick; the questions bland and generic. I was also tired of the same ol' approach to these books. You know what I mean – chapter devoted to a single animator, tell the reader where the artist was born, educated, how they came to animation and then take them through each of their films, providing description and analysis.

Yawn.

This book does not follow that pattern. Instead, I've gutted that structure, removed "facts" about the animators and cut to the point by writing somewhat stream-of-consciousness impressions about the artists and their films.

Some of you will undoubtedly find this approach a tad different, but it's my belief that this method can better capture the essence of the subject than a conventional linear biographical method.

Although I studied cultural theory, philosophy and sociology at university, I despise academic writing. I found the writing condescending as though academics and students were racing to outdo each other with the latest cryptic words and baffling French theories. They wrote as if the artist never existed. The texts became more about the academic removal of the art and artist from the context of their time and randomly placing a quilt of cultural theory over them. These works became more about the academic theory than the artist.

The main thing that annoyed me was that these ideas were not reaching anyone outside of academia. Why are they speaking to each other? How is that benefiting society? What IS the point?

Being young and impressionable I initially embraced this dry style so I could impress my classmates and professors . But the style just didn't feel right to me. It felt dishonest. Half the time I had no idea what I was saying or thinking.

A few years after graduating, I was hit by a big blast of fresh air courtesy of 1970s music critics. They wrote in a very direct, emotional and intelligent way. They spoke to real people and placed the works in the context of their time. You also didn't need Raymond William's cultural jargon dictionary, Keywords, to decipher these texts.

My approach here (and in most of my other books) is by no means new. As my friend, American animator David Ehrlich, wrote to me: "Late 19th century and early 20th century art criticism, especially by British writers, was essentially impressionistic, poetic at times, but also a bit mushy and amorphous. The last 70 years of criticism have been in various forms a means of clearing away the excesses of impressionistic writing and getting back to the text. At this point, textual analysis has swung in the opposite direction, removing from consideration any discussion of the creator of that text or the processes by which the text may have been created."

My writing strives to place the artists back in the game as the creators of their work. The means by which I do this is quite personal. It is an extrapolation of what I think the artist sees by a phenomenological analysis of what I see and think.

"Watch out for intellect", said poet Anne Sexton, "because it knows so much it knows nothing and leaves you hanging upside down, mouthing knowledge as your heart falls out of your mouth". *Time out of Mind* is fuelled not by intellect , but by instinct, emotion and honesty – however faulty. I'm hopeful that you're able to view these works and artists in terms that I think the artist has seen it in their mind's eye.

So, there you go. You've been warned. Consider this work a fictional non-fiction or a non-fictional fiction. It's your choice. Choice is important, essential even.

This book should not be interpreted as a complete overview of Japanese animators. The choices here are completely subjective – sometimes based on the availability of films. There are many other important independent Japanese animators past, present and future. My apologies to those who have been overlooked.

So, strap yourselves in, relax and just go with the rhythm of the ride.

Chris Robinson
Ottawa, Canada

Chris Robinson and Nobuaki Doi present: An Extremely Brief, Unsexy and Dry History of Independent Japanese Animation

Seems that Japan gave birth to animation around 1907. According to Jasper Sharp in his 2005 article, "The First Frames of Anime", a three-second strip of celluloid (must have been a riveting film) estimated to be made circa 1907, is thought to be Japan's first animation film.

The first animation of any substance is believed to have been The Janitor (1917) credited to Hekoten Shimokawa. Two other animators (Junichi Kouchi and Seitaro Kitayama) are also believed to have made films that same year.

Kitayama is arguably the most important of the three. In 1921, he founded Japan's first animation studio, Kitayama Eiga Seisakusho. The studio churned out animation shorts, commercial films, educational works and sequences for live-action films.

The late 1920s and early 1930s saw the emergence of three of the biggies of the era: Kenzo Masaoka, Noburo Ofuji and Yasuji Murata. Inspired by manga and Japanese folk tales, the holy trinity and others created animation works that rivaled anything coming from the good ol' U.S. of A.

Masaoka was considered a kind of Walt Disney of Japanese animation. His modern production innovations eventually led to the beginnings of Japanese anime (starting with the famous Toei animation studio in the 1950s).

The Second World War was a low point for Japanese animation (and, well, Japan in general). Film stock was hard to get and the Japanese government primarily funded animated propaganda films. Even some feature propaganda films were made, including Momotaro's Gods-Blessed Sea Warriors, which was directed by Seo Mitsuo (with the help of his master Masaoka).

On the other hand, Ofuji is the grandfather of independent animation in Japan. He established his own company and made animation films independently until the late 1950s. His most acclaimed films (*Whale*, 1927, *Ghost Ship*, 1956,) won prizes at Cannes and Venice, respectively.

Masaoka and Ofuji took two very different roads. Having little interest in commercial animation (there is already a bevy of writing about that stuff), this book will follow the indie path paved by Ofuji.

Modern independent Japanese animation has its roots in the 1950s. In 1958, Sogetsu Art Centre was founded at the Sogetsu Hall. Many hip, beret-wearing, avant-garde artists – including filmmakers and animators – gathered there. Experimental and avant-garde films were shown, including the films of Canadian animator, Norman McLaren. These films jolted the artists from their post-war slumber, notably Yoji Kuri (the father of modern independent animation in Japan). Along with Hiroshi Manabe, a painter, and Ryohei Yanagihara, a designer, Kuri formed a group called "Animation Sannin no Kai" (The Group of Three Animators) in 1960. The trio made films independently and screened them in the Sogetsu Hall. In 1964, the trio started "Animation Festival" in Sogetsu. The festival played a major role in starting the world of personal animation in Japan. This first big wave of indie animation in Japan came to its ending in 1971 when the Sogetsu art centre closed.

The 1960s saw an explosion (boom!) in Japanese animation production. Commercial animation was being produced on a large-scale and animators like Osamu Tezuka, Kihachiro Kawamoto, Tadanari Okamoto and Yoji Kuri began producing independent short films. These independent artists (and others) either worked in their own home studios or established small boutique studios that combined commercial and artistic work. Kawamoto and Okamoto learned to make wooden figures come to life from the puppet master, Tadahito Mochinaga.

Independent animation lost its energy in the 1970s. Okamoto and Kawamoto started the mostly annual screening event "Puppet Animashow" in 1972, but other than them, there were few active independent animators: among them Taku Furukawa, Sayoko and Renzo Kinoshita, Nobuhiro Aihara etc.

The Japan Animation Film Association was founded in 1978. Their workshops paved the way for the second wave of indie animation in the 1980s.

Another important group was Image Forum, which focused primarily on avant-garde and experimental films, including animation. Even though the people who established Image Forum were not animators, its school still produced many independent animators.

In the 1980s, the Hiroshima animation festival also stimulated a new generation of artists. The festival, created by Sayoko and Renzo Kinoshita provided a space for Japanese animators to screen their works and meet their contemporaries. The festival also introduced a wealth of international animation shorts to Japanese audiences.

Art students from around Japan formed many screening groups. (Indie Japanese animators love forming groups.) With 8mm film being cheap to use, many new animators emerged, triggering a second wave of independent animation in Japan.

The second wave subsided in the 1990s. While there were innovative commercial films (notably MTV Japan and its later incarnation, Vibe) achieving international success, there were few Japanese independent films of interest. On the other hand, the world of commercial animation (e.g. anime, Hayao

Miyazaki) flourished and received national and international attention.

The two major independent animators of this period are Keita Kurosaka and Koji Yamamura. Their films were well received internationally, winning various awards. Unfortunately, no one in Japan noticed their success (yet another example of the lack of respect given to artistic animation). The first time indie animation got nationwide attention came when Yamamura's Atama Yama (2002) received an Oscar nomination. Even if so, when the film won a grand prize at the famous Annecy animation festival in 2003, almost no one paid any notice.

In the '00s indie animation returned from the dead. Technological developments democratized animation, opening the door for faster and more affordable production methods. The Internet freed some animators from producers and distributors. Artists could now make their own DVDs, put their films on You Tube or set up websites. These innovations let animators (and filmmakers in general) eliminate the middle man and gave them direct contact with their audience. Responding to the new-found interest in artistic animation, a number of animation schools and animation departments opened during this period. The result was a dramatic increase in indie animation production. Today, indie animation in Japan has never been so alive and active.

Like every country, independent animation struggles in Japan. Funding is, and always will be, a challenge for esoteric, personal films that exist in a world that sees animation as little more than entertainment for children and teens. So far that hasn't stopped artists (e.g. Atsushi Wada, Maya Yonesho, Kei Oyama) from creating stimulating new work that continues to expand the vocabulary of artistic animation.

Shadows Are Falling

The dead of winter came early. A week from Christmas, temperatures brutally cold. I'm walking along a street heading to pick up my son from daycare. He's late finishing, so I roam around the neighbourhood while I wait. I struggle to stay warm. The cold slices through my cheap jacket. Fingers rolled into my palm to keep them from snapping. Ears are burning. Keep walking. See some guys looking mysterious at the side of a house. Wonder if it's a drug house. Fingers are going to crack off. I hate the winter. Harry's finally ready to go. We head home.

Phone ringing.

"Are you sitting down? You need to be sitting down."

I feel a chill blast through my body.

"Barry had a heart attack last night. He's dead."

Silence. Numb. Words are heard, but not understood. Have to say something. What? What can I possibly say? Words fall out.

"No ... no ... "

More silence. What do I do? I want to know more. Can I ask?

"I think I'd like you to speak at the funeral."

"Umm ... of course. Just let me know."

"I can't believe this has happened. Where has my husband gone?"

I have nothing to say. I don't know what to say. Numb. Frozen. Lost.

"Just let me know when the funeral will be. I'll talk with you soon, OK?"

Long silence. Sobs.

I turn the phone off and just stare out our too big living room window at nothing. Maybe it's like that moment when you wake up and haven't quite found your bearings, unsure of where or what.

What do I do now? What am I supposed to do?

I email Barry and tell him that I'll miss him and that I love him.

?

Barry was my best friend. No, in fact, he was my brother. We'd known each other almost 30 years. We went to school together, worked together and started a band together. After a few years apart, we reconnected, this time as husbands and fathers. Our friendship became stronger than ever.

I sink.

A constant ache in the stomach. Spontaneous bursts of sobbing. Hurts so much. I see and hear him all the time. Can't get him out of my head. Maybe I don't want to. I think he's coming back. No. Not fair. Not right. Worry about my mortality. Am I next? Is that a pain in my chest? Christ. Going nutty. What's the point, then? What is the damn point? Writing for what? Doesn't mean a thing. Yeah, cliché nihilism. Sorry. No, wait, I'm not. Eat me.

Visitation. Funeral. Christmas. New Year's. Blur.

I'm heading to Japan. Not sure I can handle it. Maybe it's good that I get away and get my crap together. I'm driving everyone crazy. Lashing out at family, friends, and strangers. Spending days in my room, sobbing, smashing and sleeping. I've already delayed the trip once. Can't do it again. Wonder if I can cancel it? No, that's stupid. This is the trip of a lifetime. First class airfare. Hotel. Translator. Escort. Two weeks to do whatever I want.

I can't go.

I go.

Tokyo Now

A month after Barry's death, I'm walking through streets of the
Tokyo airport.

"Ohio!" says the voice from the airline.

Why do they keep saying that? Are they asking me about Ohio?
Is there a sizeable Japanese community there? Can't imagine
why. Who the heck wants to live in Cleveland or Cincinnati?
Dayton is cool. Robert Pollard comes from there.

I return a half smile of the decomposed.

Clear customs.

No one to greet me.

Find a bench, I sit, wait and try to understand.

Big Bird walks by and nods.

I don't nod back.

He looks lost.

Young guy sitting beside me. Dressed semi-formally in dress
pants, shirt and tie. Acting a bit odd. Seems to be sniffing a lot.
At first I thought he had a cold, then I notice that he's sniffing
everything around him. He notices me looking at him and says,

わ た し の 名前 **Atsushi Wada."**

What?

Whatever.

Figure 1.
Manipulated Man.

He takes the top of his head off and invites me inside.

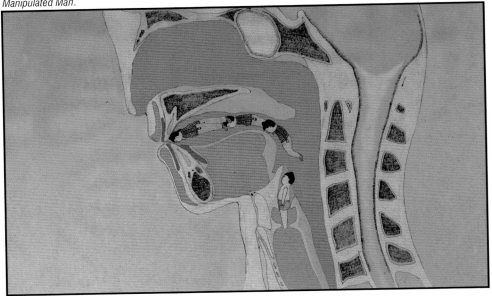

I accept.

He can't draw very well.

What does that even mean?

What does it mean to draw well? Is there some sort of bible that says, "OK, here's how it is". I guess there is if you ask those twit gag cartoonists. If it ain't Preston Blair, it ain't underwear.

Whatever. Those twit cartoonists are mostly robots. I know this guy named Pistol PeteY. He makes this real boring artwork. Squirrels and lizards and caricatures of barely-celebrities. Heck, he reminds me of Wada's friends. He keeps going through the same motions without ever stopping to consider that maybe there are different ways of doing IT.

I don't like guys like Pistol PeteY. They live in caves with Plato seeing only fragments of the world, familiar shadows that keep them safe and warm on a cold winter night in January.

Figure 2. *Day of Nose.*

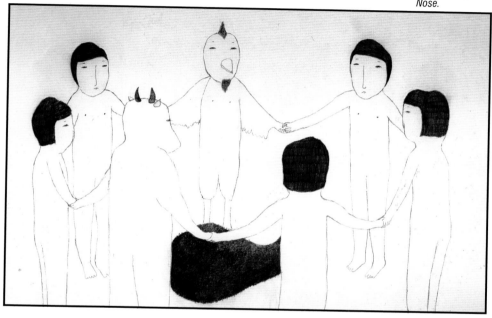

Wada's voice interrupts.

A Modigliani-like woman stands and stares at us for 10 seconds, then she turns her face back. "I didn't want to depict the act of looking back itself, nor to show what she saw after looking back. What I wanted to express was the atmosphere or the feeling of (tension in) the interval until she looked back … Such interval is called 'Ma' in Japanese. (Japanese traditional art such as 'Noh' or 'Rakugo' has the same notion.) 'Ma' is the most important point in my works. So my work doesn't necessarily need to be animation if I can express 'Ma.' Animation is better than live-action because in animation I can draw everything on a screen. (In live-action everything will be on a screen once I shoot.) In other words, in animation I don't have to draw anything if I don't want to! So I started to animate my scribble-like drawings."

11

It's cold here. Snow falling in Tokyo. Is that normal?

I wonder if Wada likes people.

A bunch of guys (all dressed nicely) throw rocks at a young man. Bruises cover his face but he doesn't complain. Eventually, the men get bored. One of them picks up a rock and tosses it at his

Figure 3.
Manipulated Man.

own face. The other men follow. Finally, the initial victim grabs a stone and follows suit.

Why does a man smack an elephant, call it "bitch" and call for birds to carry the massive animal off to another destination? When the man rejects one of the elephants, the man is swallowed (voluntarily) by the one-time bitch. A moment passes until another man arrives and repeats the actions of the first man.

Then there are the guys – they're all guys, aren't they? Maybe gals are smarter – who follow their noses. They play a form of musical chairs (except there's no music). The man at the end of the row of chairs has his nose pinched by the man standing. Nose pinched, the man stands up and walks toward a wall, sniffs it and momentarily enters some sort of fantasy world littered with dreamlike characters and possibilities. Then it stops. The man returns to his place in the line. The game goes on.

Figure 4. *Well That's Glasses.*

This is actually pretty funny stuff. Maybe Wada does like folks. Perhaps he's just a heh-hey guy, a sort of intellectual Beavis and Butthead. Can't help but be funny when you see a guy do a sort of partial Elaine Benes (*Seinfeld* reference, kids) dance that sends a half dozen or so tiny birds off with a massive elephant. He seems to see the comedy underneath the pained existence.

Wada's voice echoes inside his head.

"I laugh at comical nature of people, who never notice the meaning of their behaviour and firmly believe that repeating such stupid acts mechanically is their work. But at the same time, I feel sympathy with the very same nature and feel sad. Sometimes I even feel love. I think *Well, that's the Glasses* is the same with other films because that this film has comicality and sadness towards such people's acts, too."

13

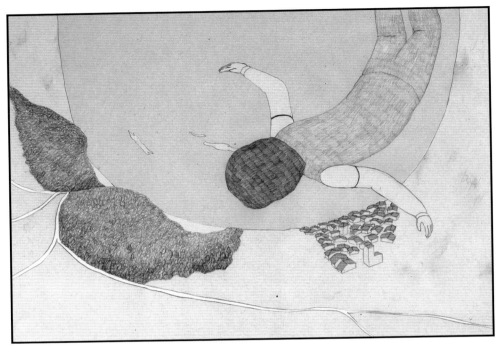

Figure 5. *Day of Nose*.

Figure 6. *Well That's Glasses*.

A hoard of Buster Keatons are dancing to the stilted rhythms of Igor Kovalyov. Stone faced fools swept into a life they don't comprehend or enjoy.

"When they face the absurd situation, they feel strange, but at the same time, they know such situation is possible even if it is strange and resign themselves to their fate. I don't think their behaviour will solve any problems and I know it can be very dangerous with such acceptance, but I like it."

For a world that seems so absurd I wonder why it looks like the world around me.

Figure 7. *Usual Sunday.*

Kei Oyama

Tokyo

Roppongi District.

Overwhelming. There's not space enough to be anywhere.

Even worse, I'm in a place where I don't where I am.

I find a hotel.

Fall asleep early. Dream loud.

A fat ugly young woman French kisses me. She whispers "Kei Oyama. Kei Oyama". The kisses become stronger. I feel myself being sucked inside her. I travel down her insides passing a stream of fish. Soon I see nothing but fish.

Fragments of light soon appear between the fish barrage. I fight through the fish and reach the light. I slip through the thin, tight, moist space and emerge into blinding light. Fish continue to race by, knocking me down. I get up and jump aside. I turn back and look up. I see a naked woman sitting in the corner of a room. Beneath her, fish enter the space I've just left: her vagina.

Mother?

Disgusted, I speed slowly out of the room. I turn and race into the first room I see. A sumo wrestler lies naked on the floor watching a game show on television. A mosquito buzzes by. I call out, but he doesn't hear me. He gets up and has a smoke, reads a magazine, cleans the room. The fly continues to buzz unnoticed. I can't leave, can't seem to move. My eyes are transfixed by the tediousness of the situation. Am I in a Chantal Akerman film?

In a flash everything changes. It's night time. I'm in a bedroom. The sumo wrestler sleeps. Flies are everywhere. The floor is littered with bottles and garbage. How can he sleep? The noise of the flies is driving me crazy. I block my ears and focus on the window. I watch the light change. Occasionally, something seems to walk by the window. I try to get to the window so that I can see what's happening, but I can't reach it. Everytime I move, the window is always out of reach. Crash. Something has fallen. The sumo wrestler wakes up and puts the fallen item back in its place. He returns to the bed. How can he not see me? Am I a ghost?

Now we're in the dining room. There are two sumo wrestlers. They are seated at a table drinking coffee.

Figure 8.
*Consultation
Room.*

One sumo wrestler leaves. The other walks back and forth anxiously. Rain pours down. Sumo wrestler returns. The other one dries his hair off. They look outside. A rainbow. Music. Dancing. Sex on the couch.

Over.

What kind of dream is this? Is it a dream? It feels too much like life – minus the naked sumo wrestlers.

"They are not sumo wrestlers", the voice says.

The voice continues: "I saw the beauty from these boring things. You can feel beauty, grotesque, sadness and comicality in

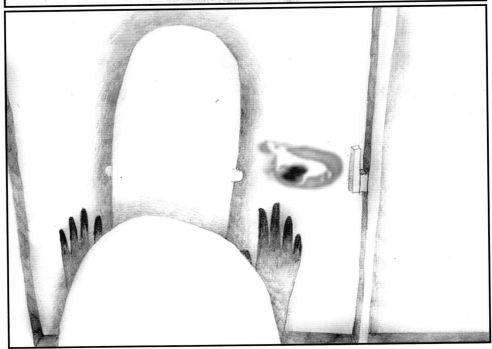

everyday life by staring at it more carefully. I love to give shape to the beauty that I discover. I also love to know the beauty which other people find and I never know."

I walk past the humping wrestlers toward the window. I look out and am startled by the sudden appearance of a skeletal figure on the other side. His hands and face are barely visible. I float through the window and discover a young man. Together we look out the window.

Spring is coming.

Everything is beginning to thaw.

A dead dog lies in the moist snow.

I watch as the boy pulls strands of hair from his head.

Bored with that he grabs a goldfish from its bowl. The fish struggles to breath. I move closer and jump inside the darkness of the fish's mouth.

Dinner time. Cut into the food. Blood and crap seeps out. As the adults eat, their faces darken. Horrified, the boy and I flee to the bedroom.

We stare out the window. I look at the boy. His face darkens and soon the entire room explodes into a silent blackness.

Out of the darkness, I see a worm. A boy pokes at it with a stick. He pauses to smash a bug on his hand.

A hand grabs the boy and rushes him to a room. A woman kneels over a dying girl. The boy strokes her head gently.

The boy is a man now. He sits silently in a doctor's office. A nurse stands nearby.

The man looks sad and anxious.

Figure 9a, b (facing). *The Thaw*.

19

A doctor arrives, places x-rays on the lightboard. Nothing is spoken, everything is said.

The man stares at the floor and scratches his knee.

I look at the spot on the X-ray and jump through it.

Figure 10. *Yuki Chan*.

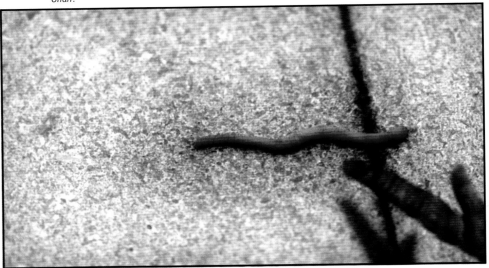

In a room I see a woman. Mother? Ugly scrunched up faces peer in the window. What's so fascinating? The woman tends to my bruised knee.

A headless fat woman sits in a cubicle. A needle enters her skin. Bruises appear all over her body.

Everything goes dark.

A curtain rises. Two boys play with a dog. The dog pees. A boy collapses to the ground. The audience laughs as a stretcher comes to take the boy away.

The boy returns to a doctor's office. It's the same scene as earlier.

The curtain closes. The actor's bow. Applause.

Doctor's office. Man scratches his knee.

A voice: "When I was a child, I often imagined such scenes and cried a lot: my mother killed herself by leaping from a window or was becoming weak from heavy illness. (Of course, these things happened just in my imagination.) When I was in my teen, I started to fear about my own death. And recently, thinking about death of people around me started to scare me again."

Figure 11. *Hand Soap*

That's all I remember. I wake up sobbing, full of melancholia. I get up, piss, and make some bad hotel room coffee.

What was that dream all about? It was so sad and weird and mundane, yet beautiful. Was it connected to Barry's death? Death and illness pervaded the dreamscape.

All the people in the dream were like ghosts. They seemed real and animated at the same time as though trapped between life and death.

I suddenly remember the last thing that mysterious voice said before I woke up:

21

"I feel as if I am not myself when my fear about death is getting bigger (it often happens when I try to sleep in my bed). Of course it is an illusion but it is a really weird feeling as if I am glancing at Kei Oyama very, very far from him and perceive him as a complete stranger. That unsettledness that these characters in your dream have is really like this strange feeling."

What's strange, too, is that the characters, while always aware of their mortality, continued on, not racing to do monumental things. Instead, they just lived the life they always did. The wrestlers just carry on with those simple, seemingly uneventful parts of their day. Maybe it's a message to stop trying to live so big and to accept the everyday, that there is life and meaning in lying on the floor and reading a magazine, a simple dance, a good lay or smoke. Moments that might be irrelevant to others, but are individual moments, our moments. Look at the dying guy. He remembered a bruised knee and a school play. They seem trivial to me, but they are clearly everything to him.

Too often we overlook and don't appreciate the usual.

Pissing down snow today. Apparently it's a cold winter here. I find it warm.

I'm walking through the streets feeling a million miles from home.

A deep booming voice interrupts my thoughts: "Chris Robinson".

I look around and just see people hurrying nowhere fast. I keep walking.

"CHRIS ROBINSON!"

I stop, look around again. Nothing.

"LOOK TO THE SKIES!"

I stop and look up and see a face inside a large grey cloud.

"I AM NAOYUKI TSUJI!"

I scratch my head and say nothing.

"YOU MUST TELL THEM ABOUT ME."

"Tell who what?"

"THE PEOPLE OUT THERE WATCHING US."

"Are you nuts? There's no one watching us. Do you see people out there watching us?"

"I SEE ALL. I SEE THE ENTIRE PICTURE. THEY ARE OUT THERE IN HOMES, PLANES, TRAINS, BUSES, SUBWAYS, TOILETS, READING THESE WORDS."

This guy's nuts, but I'm not about to argue with a giant face in a grey cloud. So, let me tell you about Naoyuki Tsuji.

Who is Naoyuki Tsuji? I dunno. Never heard of him before. Guess he doesn't do animation festivals. Where was he born? Does it matter? Do you want to know? I can find out. Hold on …

Someone I don't know says it's 1972. I'll take his word for it. Make "you" feel better?

Oh, he's Japanese. I bet you guessed that already, though.

Does this tell you enough? Do you feel you know him better?

Do you wonder if he's tall or short, thin or fat? What's his favorite colour, favourite song? Where does he live? Is there more than one guy in the world with his name? Does he eat cheese? Can he dance? Does he have legs (one of his characters has no arms)? Can he drive? Did he make me cry once?

Does it matter? Will those things help you know Tsuji any better? Is there a self we can even know? David Hume said that self was nothing but a bundle of different perceptions. So

23

identity depends on which given perception is on stage. I know enough to say that for me Naoyuki Tsuji is the author of *Wake Up* (1992) and *A Feather Stare in the Dark* (2003). However, I can't say that the same Naoyuki Tsuji made these films. Get my drift?

Figure 12. *Trilogy about Clouds*.

What does Tsuji think about his films? Doesn't matter. They're not his anymore. He already said them once.

Besides, how much can we rely on his memory as truth? I'm constantly wondering if the loud visions I keep of childhood really existed or if they were stories I pieced together through home movies, slides or old photos. I'm sure I think I experienced events that I didn't. How much of our memory is ours anyway? How much of another's memories do we take on that become fragments of our own?

Popeye always bragged that "I yam what I yam". No, sorry matey, I think Posh Spice – who knows quite a thing or three about image and identity – said it best when she stunned a

Young Girls for America Philosophy Fashion conference in Syracuse, New York, by telling them "I am as I am not".

David Beckham, her learned man, who studies the pre-Socratics when he can, once told his cleated mates before the match of

Figure 13. *Trilogy about Clouds.*

matches that the way up is the way down, the straight and curved line are one and the same, and that the best we can do is expect the unexpected. Wise words from a man who knows of what he speaks.

"It's random, yet with direction, ordered towards the future. I start with no set idea for the film. Each image I draw and photograph creates suggestions which lead to the next image, and these images build up inside me as the film advances.

Tsuji said that.

"Go at it slow. Sit back. Take it in. Don't fight. Just flow."

I said that.

"I'll let you be in my dreams, if I can be in yours"

Bob Dylan said that.

Figure 14. *A Feather Stare at the Dark.*

A friend of mine says I am what I am. It ain't right. Can't be AM cause you always ARE – at least till you AIN'T. Are is in the process. Am is always shifting. And what you are might not jive with those who know you. Who says your ARE is more valid than their ARE? AM(s) is always with the ARE.

Ghost, reminders, memories, past breaths.

I like this guy Tsuji. He's everything I like about the best animation. His work is primitive kind of ugly, but not in some accidental sloppy way. This guy knows what he's doing, sort of like he's frantically scribbling to try and keep up with the world. As he draws one conclusion, another immediately appears and on it goes. Yet as he keeps going forward, shadows of what he

26

has learned remain, they are never entirely forgotten. They move forward with each new bit of knowledge.

Tsuji's drawing style looks like a kid's. Quickly, defenders of ART race to clarify that in fact Tsuji's work is anything BUT

Figure 15.
Children of
Shadows.

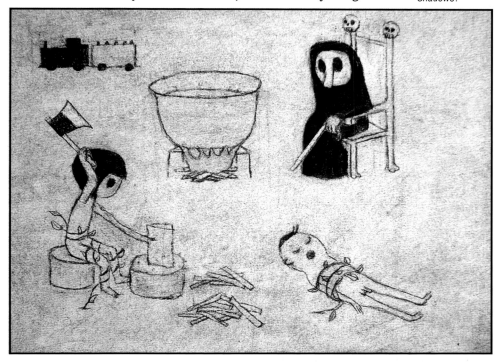

childish. Nonsense says me. Such an insult to the kids (our future). I have kids. They sometimes see the world in a clearer and more profound way than most of us so-called adults. The other day Jarvis, (my 9 year old), said that priests are the same as shrinks. Pretty spot on I'd say. Most adults wouldn't pick that up. No, I say that Tsuji's drawings are like those of kids. His scribbles and thoughts are as simple, profound and stupid as any kid's doodles. That's what makes them so interesting, inviting and warmer than films by the brothers Kray and Wankmajer.

Tsuji's got rhythm too. I said Tsuji's got rhythm too. It ain't no Fred and Ginger swing. It's "the swing of the Earth". Characters move about awkwardly, cautiously, to and fro without control. It's sort of an Albert Ayler kinda (anti-) groove. Tsuji's just looking down at that paper and making up the notes with each touch push and shove of the charcoal. It's that attempt at real-time simulation (let's face it kids, animation can't be in real time, now can it?) that grounds the work, keeps it from getting too precious and artsy fartsy. Instead, it feels like life, like a guy who craps like me and "you" (I know who I am, but I don't

Figure 16. Trilogy about Clouds.

know "you" or "you"). Some of the images are logical, pleasing and insightful, others are just plain surprising, painful and ridiculous. It's like seeing the highs and lows of a naked man, naughty bits and all. Tsuji ain't no prude.

Breathing cloud. Cloud grows. Mountains fade. Shadows remain. Cloud expands to take over the whole frame. Forms a hand, then faces. Kids snort clouds, get naked and have a ball. A couple make love, then child, then they close their eyes and fade into the cloud. Tsuji never let's us forget that the universe and the STUFF of us is transient and fragile. Here today, gone tomorrow. But it ain't so bad for Tsuji. He embraces and relishes the uncertainty of our blip of an existence. Man woman boy birds devils clouds dicks death. All part of the same volcano ("flesh quakes") of this thing we call living.

Tsuji's embrace of – even enthusiasm for – the unknown keeps us calm. Unlike the overwhelming chaos of Ayler's often

Figure 17.
Children of
Shadows.

piercing, violent sounds, you feel somehow at ease in Tsuji's world. There is something comforting about the chaos. No matter how far into wackyland it strays, you always feel connected. Nothing ever engulfs you as you pass through the torn formations of the shadow ghosts from was and were.

Let's not forget the music either. Minimalist peeps that stay back and observe, reminding us of our own fleeting PEEP-ness. It's there, then gone – but, oh so gently, like the wind outside my door right now that's whispering humid.

But do we see, hear, feel? Are we more consumed with our dreams than our reality? Does it matter? If reality is just a fleeting dream, then so be it. Who gives a fug what your truth is?

Just be, and flow with the it (which is where we'll all end up anyway, ain't it?) Like my pals Philip and Thomas said, you aint gonna find no salvation in the clouds, you ain't gonna find no big-ass bearded man waiting to welcome you through the gates (well, except for my hermit neighbour Paul who lives in an old church). You're it. You're all. You're nothing. You're

Figure 18. *A Feather Stare at the Dark.*

everything. You ARE it. IT you are. So be IT. So it BE. You're free to BE.

SCAR-Y.

("Ain't dat da tooth", said a rascal.)

This is good stuff, kids. Forget all that precious, lovey-dovey, it's gotta be drawn and design and executed with the precision of a robot and the grace of a dancer. That stuff ain't for me. There ain't no RIGHT way to do animation, to do art. Tsuji brings a much needed blast of Beat spirit to an artform that needs less adults and more raw powered punks.

Tsuji's work celebrates the dream of reality and the reality of the dream that will end sometime down the road. He draws us into a black and white world that is in fact never black and white.

?

Getting to know Naoyuki Tsuji:

Tsuji is taller than Paul Simon, but shorter than Steve Coogan.

He can drive a bicycle.

He likes some cheeses, but not others.

He didn't make me cry yet, but he probably will.

His favourite colour is grey ("where the action is" he told me once – in a dream)

There is a Naouki Tsuji was president of Hudson Soft USA.

When he dances he feels as though he only has one leg.

Loves the song *Talkin' World War 3 Blues*

He was born in Shizuoka, a city famous for its green tea.

"That's all I've got."

"IT IS GOOD. THANK YOU."

The cloud suddenly twists and twirls with blinding speed. Like a whirlpool it closes in on itself. Soon there is nothing, but blue sky.

I lower my head and continue my walk, but not before smacking into a young man. He carries a beautiful swirling disc in his hand.

31

Figure 19. *Jam*.

Figure 20. *Lost Utopia*.

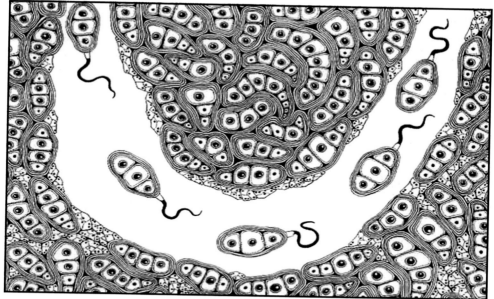

Figure 21. *Fantastic Cell*.

Figure 22. *Lost Utopia*.

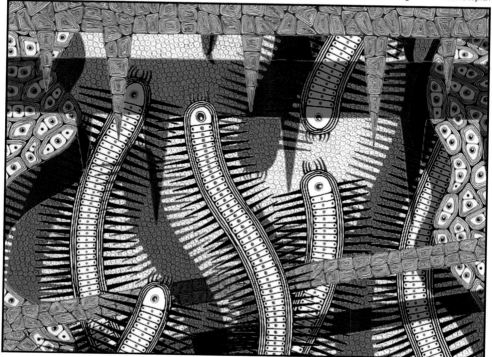

Figure 23. *Devour Dinner*.

"I am **Mirai Mizue**. Please look into my disc."

The disc is hypnotic, composed of a maze of multi-coloured shapes that seem to flow in and out of each other. I find myself getting increasingly lost along the path of the drawings. I move closer and find myself devoured by a kaleidoscope of colour. Suddenly, a young girl greets me. "Will you marry me?" Her hat suddenly expands into a garden of colours.

She is gone before I can answer.

"I'm really interested in myself: Of what am I made?" Mirai Mizue whispers. "My body consists of 60 trillion cells, but I am always wondering which cells are allotted to be my mind, soul or feelings? I feel sure that there are other things in myself other than cells. Some invisible elements. Not visible elements like cells, but invisible elements that make us create something like society, culture, songs, drawings or something like that."

I am swept along a path before I can choose. Initially, there are few paths to follow, but soon new roads appear, intersecting, overlapping. A crush of colours

A distinctive, recurring image of a rectangular shape with what looks like an eye inside it. Is the eye a cel, revealing the interior of human and all things? Creatures and people roam around me beyond naked. No flesh. I feel like I'm seeing the world through a kaleidoscopic microscope, seeing deeper than my eyes often show me. X-rays, showing the essence of our bodies. See-through figures. Everything flows in and out of each other, ultimately one. In this randomness rests chaos and order.

A voice: "Then after desire has conceived, it gives birth to sin, and sin, when it is full grown, gives birth to death".

Apple as sin. Everyone eats a part of the apple. We all sin. It's inescapable.

Figure 24. *Lost Utopia*.

Mizue nods: "Sin is inescapable even though there are some people who are not conscious about it. Criminal laws are for deeds, but sin is a natural element of oneself. This is one of the

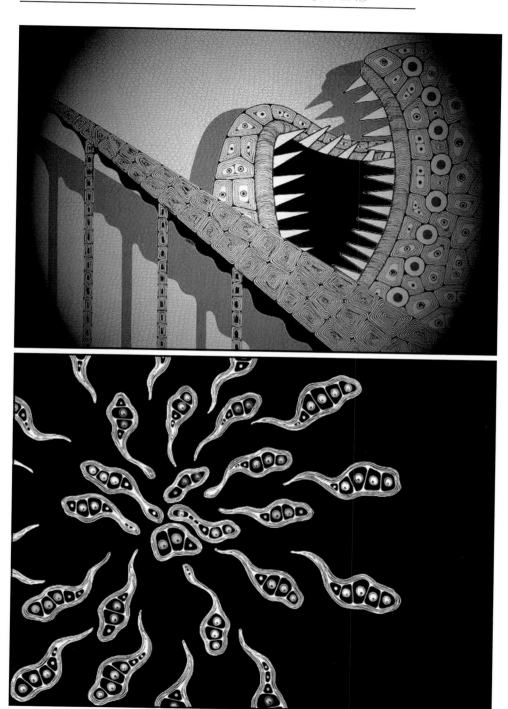

invisible elements that I spoke of, I think. There are always discussions about our nature: are we fundamentally good or bad? My answer is neither. Humanity is an incomplete existence."

Figure 25.
Adamski.

Our lives are spent devouring. We eat and are eaten. Food is birth and death. The birth of eater, the death of the eaten. "To eat means to kill", Mizue says. "This act is continued repeatedly daily and unconsciously. You never finish it unless you live. To live means to kill. You can see the same structure everywhere from the microscopic world where amoebas live to the society we live."

Blending in and out each other. The randomness of these connections. Randomness of birth. Being born, a miracle really. The odds are so high against your existence ... of EACH existence.

"Right", Mizue says. "The world is nothing, but order and chaos. Without collapsing. (It's possible that we are slowly reaching a state of collapse ...) I can see them in the history of humanity, in my life, in the cells that a body consists of."

Trees, stones and grass dance, jump, move.

Cities move. Colour, shapes, order.

Tedious.

Unchanging.

"I can see the chaos in the world I live (Tokyo) when I look down the city from the top of a skyscraper. It's not possible if I am *in* the world. From this perspective though, I can understand the place I am in. Roads have many branches that get in between buildings and on them there are so many cars running. They are like blood vessels and bloodstreams. It seems to me that the more I look outside, the more I understand inside myself. Maybe this is because me and the world outside are not completely separated, that we are related to each other. Like a human body is consisted of 60 trillion cells, and a human being is one of the many cells that consist of the world, I think."

Transient permanence. Permanent transience.

Society changes as we change.

Nature, hobbled and broken, remains.

A young girl looks over at me and speaks: "**Keita Kurosaka** is expecting you".

I remember Kurosaka, or rather his short film *Flying Daddy*. Played at our festival in the late 1990s. Something about kids going to wake their daddy up, but finding a grotesque creature à la Kafka under the bed. The shelled creature suddenly comes to life. Daddy emerges with wings and briefcase and flies out the window, joining the other flying pops on their way to work.

Beyond that I only know that Kurosaka was one of the two animators (the other being Koji Yamamura) who helped rejuvenate indie animation in Japan during the 1990s.

Figure 26. *Sea Roar.*

The girl, meanwhile, is pale and ghostly with barely eyes. As she moves closer her faces jolts and shifts, morphing into a ghostly face struggling to form. Stretching and pulling and shifting. Bill Plympton in hell. Fat grotesque faces.

Figure 27. *Haruko Adventure.*

I wonder what kind of guy Kurosaka is? Seemed mild mannered when I met him briefly. Sure hope that his films are a way of unleashing his cynical violent perceptions of the world. If not, be scared. Be very scared.

A voice: "When I had a open talk with a famous psychologist, she told me that I get a catharsis and peace of mind by changing my evil energy into creation. It is possible that I draw what scares my identity most in a very paradoxical way. I am threatened by 'right' people. They never forgive others' mistakes. They demonstrate their unbelievable cruelty towards 'not right' people or things that are not useful. There is nothing more scary than the violence of justice. Essentially everyone has a craziness in their mind. It doesn't always lead them to disgusting crimes. If you release it in a positive way, it gives you energy toward your life."

His early films are more experimental than animation. LONG films using xeroxed photographs. Confusing, seemingly non-linear imagery of a dark abandoned world of memory, pain, violence, lust and loss. People lose landscapes, traditions, and lovers. The characters are disconnected from their environments, often left with scattered memories of what once was. A nerdy otaku man (pre-Internet) experiences the world through a box. A woman sees the ghosts of a destroyed housing area. A fishing village is abandoned.

Suddenly, Kurosaka's work shifts to beautifully detailed drawings of the grotesque, morphing in and out. Nothing, no one in place. Shifting. Changing. Revealing.

"My desire to create begins to turn to a 'human drama.' It made my previous method, shooting photograph frame by frame, invalid. People who are cut from a photograph are originally from reality. This makes them less alive when they are put into animation. They become a human-shaped object. This method is very suitable to make up 'a miniature of a view of the world,' but prevents viewers from empathizing with characters, so it is not good for a drama that develops around the emotion of characters. With drawings I can make characters … turn into real existence by giving them movement."

39

The world turns. A bell rings. A chorus of angels turns to haunting moans of hell. A dirty, grey world of mystery and paranoia. Shadowy figures. No one is what they seem. Monsters lurk within in us all. An insect craps. Souls burning. Tension. Fear. Silence. Creepy old man, fish monsters, devoured. Darkness. Silence. "It is highly possible that this expression is my love in a paradoxical way. In most cases, they are very close people like my family and friends. The giant old man who was born from the maggot is my grandfather who passed away 30 years ago. He was not a monster. He loved me very much when I was a child. But the memory of the past is essentially an enclosed world. If a memory is just beautiful, it will gradually fade. I cannot stand it. This is why I made him the incarnation of aggressive energy. It makes him newly alive in my memory."

"Father? Father? Where are you?"

I roll back the covers of his bed and find a bloody creature rolling around. Suddenly, it morphs into a winged man-creature who flies off to work with the other winged papas.

Figure 28. *Personal City.*

Figure 29. *Agitated Scream of Maggots.*

Figure 30. *Head.*

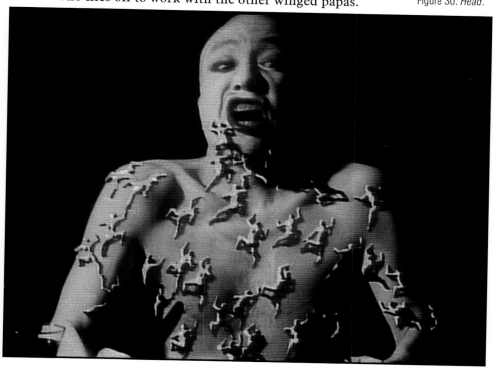

Creatures lurk behind everything. In a flash, they break free and consume my head until it bursts and explodes.

Figure 31. *Worm Story.*

I scream. My head, is it still in place?

This is a horrifying, violent world. Is it really so bad? Does everyone contain a black heart?

Man seeks water. He cups some water and sees a pair of eyes staring at him. Joy of madness. Madness of joy.

Dirty brown repulsive faces. Screams and pain. Then sky and birds. Released from pain.

Loud, damn awful speed metal drowns my ears. Maggots being sliced, morphing. The little girl walks by and crushes the humping maggot men. The maggot man grows large and defecates on the little girl. She recovers and tortures the maggot man. A woman's image rises out of the maggot man's guts. The girl smiles. "Mother?" In a flash, the girl puts her hat on and cranks a giant boot that smashes down on the maggot man.

The girl returns, face against the wall, hands over eyes. She turns. Eyes wide open. She has finally SEEN.

A man struggles to breathe. Woman lunges at him. Is she trying

Figure 32. *The Diary of Tortov Ruttle.*

to give or take his breath? They struggle and merge. One.

I close my eyes and scream. "Enough! No more. Take me away from this world. This is not the way things are. This is not the way things have to be. The world is better than this. People are not that black at heart. They are not beasts of sickness, murder and sin."

Running, I shout back at the girl, "This is not the world I live in! This is not the world I want!"

I take a subway toward the Sumida river then hop on a boat. It's warmer now. Sun fights to come out of the stubborn clouds.

43

We drift.

The tour guide prattles on as we pass by the Tsukiji fish market and the Asahi Beer building that's made in the shape of a beer glass. We go under bridge after bridge after bridge.

I lose focus and drift.

I imagine drowning. The water swallowing me as I swallow it.

Do I concede or swim on like the old man in **Kunio Kato's** film, building cube upon cube upon cube to escape the rising waters?

He's won an Oscar already. I don't think much of Oscars. It's a watered-down field of submissions. Still, it's a pretty impressive achievement for a relatively new kid on the block (ha ha, get it? block = cube. GENIUS!)

Figure 33. *House of Small Cubes.*

I remember his early films. Always felt there was something special there. Didn't always select his work for the Ottawa festival, somehow it didn't quite seem to achieve what it set out to. Maybe I was wrong? Watching films during the blur of selection differs from a more subdued, contemplative viewing.

The Diary of Tortov Ruddle. Young man dressed in tall hat, coat and scarf rides around land on his long legged horsy pig. Like Alice, Tortov wanders through dreamscapes encountering rabbit people, movie goers, a city of lights that rests upon a giant frog. Fish swim in his coffee. Bad dreams take the form of a balloon

Figure 34. *The Diary of Tortov Ruddle.*

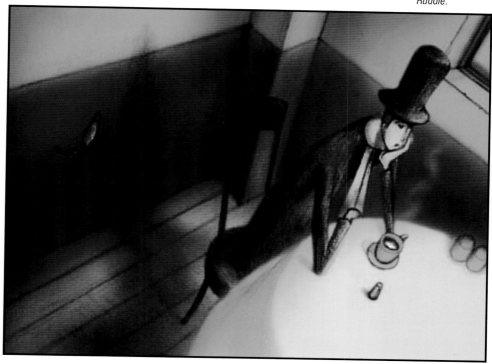

on his head. When released to sky, they create rain. Tortov meets a woman in a station. She throws him a flower. Now they're in a field. Love. Lost. He's alone with his pig around an extinguished fire. He eats fruit that gets him stoned. Meets a man dressed as a rabbit. They chase a fairy and do an assortment of things that stoned people do. Wakes up. Moves on. Another experience.

There's a gentle, warm melancholic air to Tortov's world. Nothing fazes him. Everything interests him. He is on a journey, but the destination is moot. The journey is his destination. Each step a moment, an experience.

Figure 35. *The House of Small Cubes.*

"Subtle spiritual change is the key for Tortov. Thinking about how to face life's moments that differ according to each episode, I put almost no expression into his face and didn't make him talk. I wanted people to feel the subtle change."

Are the experiences real or imagined?

"I wanted to resist the trend of emphasis on reality. I thought that it is too simplistic to decide the answer when 'reality' itself became difficult to define."

They are. That's all.

Alice takes shape in the *Fantasy* series. Tall thin girl with blue dress and red shoes. A joyful shower of leaves. Gazes with wonder at passing birds. Dances through the post-shower sun. Gapes at the fish as they seem to fly to the moon.

Early film, *Apple Incident*. Harsher colours. Rougher design. Giant apples fall. People are confused, scared. They cut them apart and eat them. Apples grow from their heads. You are what you eat.

The big one. Hollywood loved it, so did Mr. Roboto. *House of Small Cubes*. Old man lives in a house of, you guessed it, cubes that springs from the water. As the water rises the man must build a new cube. His room is modest. Wife is dead. Daughter has grown. He is alone with memories. A door on the floor leads down to the previous cube. The man gets a scuba suit and begins

Figure 36. *The House of Small Cubes.*

diving. With each cube he uncovers a memory. The farther down he swims, the deeper into the past the memories take him. Sees his sick wife. His grandchildren. Daughter getting married. Young daughter. First meeting with his wife when he was a boy. Building a home together. He returns to the top pours two glasses of wine and toasts his wife, his life.

The cubes are memories, experiences, blocks of our lives. The water, time. Slowly flooding us. Can rise above it for only so long. Then it swallows us into memory.

"Stacking up the cubes on top of each other is the only thing he can do. He needs not only memories to do this but also pride, ego, and resignation or determination. It is a grand theme to think of 'all things must pass.' I thought that the important thing is to move on even if you are filled with a sense of emptiness."

Barry didn't even have a chance. The old man had many cubes. Barry had just a few. He'd barely started. His daughters are so young. Will they remember him? Will their cubes contain him or will he be only a faint, passing impression, a shadow?

Kato is the sentimentalist of the pack. He wants us to cry and we do. How can you not? It's why Hollywood folks liked it. They like to cry, makes 'em feel alive. Kato knows the secret. Packs his films with the gentle swaying sounds of the piano. Sweet, yet haunting, keys that load the tear ducts, readying them for action.

Sepia, teal and eton blue adorn the soft, pencilled landscapes and characters.

Animation drifts patiently, deliberately.

The films can be mushy, but the emotions are genuine, like that of a child. So much innocence and joy and imagination. Kato's characters possess rich imaginations. They're always open for business, eager to taste new experiences and journeys.

Not my world, but one I wish for.

The boat docks. Lost in thought, I missed everything.

Tokyo Godfathers

The Japanese are nuts about baseball. This stadium hosts the Yomiuri Giants. As I circle the stadium, I run into animator **Taku Furukawa**, wearing a New York Yankees jersey and cap. He is baseball crazy.

"You're right on time", Taku says.

"What? I don't recall a scheduled meeting."

"Well, you're here so you must have known."

"Perhaps it was in the schedule. Oh well, that's very strange, but who cares. I'm here."

"Japanese have been playing baseball since 1935", he tells me. "Before the Meiji restoration, the western idea of sport was unheard of in Japan. During Meiji's reign, Western sport became increasingly popular, especially baseball."

Furukawa takes me inside the empty stadium. We grab a couple of seats along the third base line. "This is the home of the famous Tokyo Yomiuri Giants. They started playing in 1935 and have won more championships than any other team. The Giants are like the Yankees of Japanese baseball."

It makes sense that Furukawa is so fascinated with this Western sport. A child of the '60s, Furukawa is of the generation of Japanese that grew up under the increasing influence of Western culture. His films repeatedly express a sort of love-hate relationship with American culture in particular.

"I like U.S. baseball. I like U.S. music. I like clam chouder. I like Vonnegut, but I don't like Oil Bandido's U.S."

"My father was a teacher and one day when I was eight years old, he brought back some press materials of Disney's *Snow White*. That was really the memorial day for me to wish to be an animator."

"When I was a child, I just watched Disney films and Fleischer brother's films, but I wasn't thinking about creating animation. I started getting interested in high school. Then at the beginning of the 1960s, I watched Norman McLaren's films and many European short animation films. That's when I started thinking that maybe I wanted to make animation."

There were no animation schools in the 1960s, so Furukawa went to university to study, logically, Spanish.

Later, he found work at a commercial animation studio that churned out mediocre TV shows. "The work was very hard. I just wanted to learn the skill."

In the early 1960s, Furukawa saw the work of animator Yoji Kuri. "I was attracted by Yoji Kuri's work and wanted to learn from him so I went to him and asked him and worked in his studio for three and a half years. After I left Kuri's story, I was on my own and had to make my own living. I do illustrations for magazines and advertisements. I earned enough money to make my own films. Other than that you can earn money doing kid's work for NHK or commercials. That's the only way and I still do that.

"In my childhood, there were so many unique heroes in Japanese baseball.

We listened to their games (using our) imagination on radio, not TV, and I collected vintage cards. Then, when I was eight years old, for the first time, I discovered Major League Baseball! One day, the first Major League Baseball team came to Japan. San Francisco Seals led by Frank O'dul in 1949.

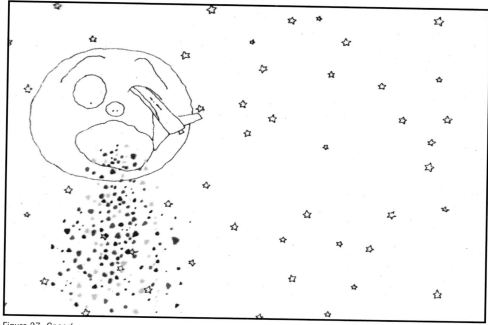

Figure 37. *Speed*.

Figure 38. Phenakistiscope.

I liked sumo, baseball and Tezuka Manga. I was living in Iga (the birthplace of ninjya) and attending Ninjya school (one of the two biggest in Japan). Everyday, I listened baseball, sumo, and American pop music from radio, with imagination. The luxury time before TV.

Figure 39. *Motion Lumine.*

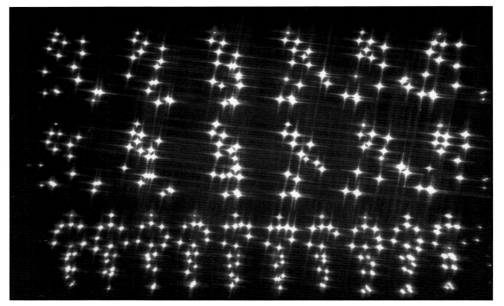

"I was in the country where there is no baseball (Portugal) when the World Series began, so I had to check live broadcasts by computer or cellphone at midnight. Thanks to the loss of Yankees in the fifth game, I could enjoy that day (when Matsui became a god) in Tokyo. I felt so pleased that I lost my wallet with 100,000 yen … but it came back to me after two days. Just great.

"I want Matsui to play in a team in the West Coast and become a home run king in MLB next year. I prefer Seattle Mariners to any other team because my relative lives there and, of course, Ichiro. I will rent my own apartment if Matsui go there! I like New York just like Matsui said in the MVP interview, but I will root for Matsui's team next year."

I don't feel well. Everything is getting blurry. Furukawa's face is changing, shifting from weird, black line drawings reminiscent of Saul Steinberg to a kaleidoscope of abstract images.

I hear the words of Furukawa? "It's all about the flicker. flicker. flicker. Flick ..." The words drift off. I don't hear him anymore. Who is he? I'm not sure. Am I seeing inside, seeing the real Furukawa? Have the percocets given me some extraordinary insight into human identity. His eye grows bigger and bigger before splitting into hundreds of little eyes.

Figure 40. *Coffee Break.*

The images seem to be from his films. There's the crazy kinetic assault of American images from *New York Trip* (1970). Then I find myself on a phenakistoscope, observing a stream of crazy imagery: sex, nudity, nature, urban landscapes. What the hell? Next, I'm in a portrait, two photographic frames. It's an anti-portrait. Not still, not a moment, but several moments, a life, lives. Constantly flowing. Nothing settles in Furukawa's films. Motion. Flux. No stability. Oh, brief break, a coffee break. Just a quiet image of a man settling down for a nice cup of coffee. A SIP and then WHAM! An explosion of colours and objects. Holy mother of god, where am I? What is happening? Is that freedom? Life? Liberated from office drab? Then the coffee cup grows bigger and swallows me. I am spit out into the sky, a glitter fest worthy of the New York dolls. Glitter stars walk and

Figure 41. *Tarzan*.

Figure 42. *Tokyo Story*.

start to look like people. *The Little Prince?* Are we always there up in the stars after we're gone?

More minimalist drawings send me through the history of the world, of food, hunting, images, technology. Each time we end up hitting the moon in the eye à la George Méliès. I keep trying to reach the unreachable. Tarzan comes to save me. He takes me

Figure 43.
Beautiful Planet.

to his gym. Feeling strong we fly to Africa and takes pictures of the wildlife. Everything we experience is through the camera. It's very strange. Why not use my eyes? We don't see much really. Everything from the top of a tour bus. Suddenly we're being watched, we're in a home movie being projected at a penthouse party. No one is interested. The man walks me to the balcony and pushes me over. I land on an eggshell man and fall off him into a computer. Slow, playful images stretch and move to the sounds of Sidney Bechet. Everything feels
Veeeeeeerrrrryyyy
Slllllllllllllllllllooooooooooooooowwwwwwwww.

I land on a boat. An old couple beside me. They tell me they're off to visit their children in Tokyo. Later we share a bullet train. As we pass Mt. Fuji, her dress lifts up à la Marilyn. The couple invites me along. I meet their son and daughter. Well, briefly. They are never still, always on the phone, work. Video games, computers, mobile phones. So much noise and distraction. No one converses. It's driving me a bit nuts. The three of us escape and walk through Tokyo. Dinner. Fireworks. Rolling Stones' concert.

Figure 44.
Jumping.

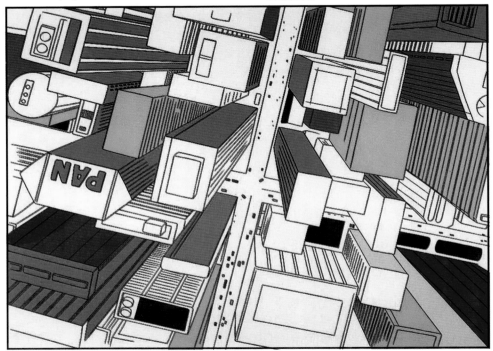

Time to go home.

Home.

Calm serenades of the water. Stillness of a sun. Everything is quiet.

Man this is boring. Forget serenity. Take me back to Tokyo.

Now I find myself running from Furukawa's films. Behind me is an animation screen. Tall woman, dinosaurs, flags, rockets all coming after me. I react to each image in confusion and absurdity.

Darkness.

Applause.

As I head back to my hotel to rest, a ghostly old man jumps out and grabs my hand.

"Don't be afraid, I am **Osamu Tezuka**."

Holding hands, we begin jumping down the street. We jump so high that I can see the rooftops of Tokyo.

Then I vomit.

We continue. "I want to show you my world."

"umm ... hey, no offence, but I'm really not interested in *Astro-Boy*, *Kimba* and all that anime crap. I'm sure kids and virgins like it, but it ain't for me, or this book."

"No, no, no ... this is a different world I live in. Few people have seen it."

Before I can respond, we are jumping again. Bouncing up and down, he shows me a man sitting, pulling hairs out. His cat is telling him off. "I am me, you are you." I only see snippets with each bounce. I can't quite figure out what's going on. The man is clearly troubled. The cat is criticizing the guy. Why can't men and women get along the way cats do? Sirens are heard. More hair is being pulled. The man is tense, anxious. A woman lies in the bed beside him, knife in back. Blood seeping.

"Umm ... that's kinda dark. You don't have much faith in humanity, do you? Cats are fighting with each other all the time. If anything, at our core we are like them, like all beasts. The man snapped and reacted like an animal. No thinking, just doing. Ain't that like an animal?"

He says nothing.

"Nice hat, gramps."

The next jump takes us from the Earth to another planet. Not quite sure what's going on. Tezuka starts talking about memory. We only remember fragments, never see the whole picture. A

Figure 45.
Memory.

man sees only women's asses and tits. When he is in love, he doesn't see other women at all. When's he dumped, he suddenly sees booty again.

Grandma is always 60 in my memory.

The girl I had a crush on in Grade 3 is always just a girl.

Our memory is faulty, fictional.

Imagine how future people/races might view us. Maybe they'll think that a toilet bowl was an essential characteristic of our life. Someone might discover one toilet and imagine that our entire society worshipped at the porcelain alter. Buildings in the form of toilets. Toilet cars. Toilet planes.

History is written by those who weren't there.

Figure 46.
Genesis.

"So what?" I ask. "Assuming there is nothing beyond our lives, who cares? What does it matter what is truth or fiction? We can learn just as much about our past, present and future from fiction. Facts don't matter. Fiction can take us beyond the facts and reveal the essence of a time and place. In fact, take this scenario between us. It is not real. I've never met you. You are dead. You are a creation of my imagination. Even the *me* in this book is fiction, an idealized persona."

We jump higher through darkness toward light. A Buddha-like figure awaits us. OK ... well ... maybe this is God. Might as well take this opportunity to speak with him.

"Barry is dead. Why did this happen? He loved life. He gave more to life than many. How tcould you steal him away from it?"

He says nothing.

"And look at this world. The suffering, violence, cruelty, wars. A world dominated by technology. Everything is mediated and provided by technology. Even people have become robots.

Figure 47. *Broken Down Film.*

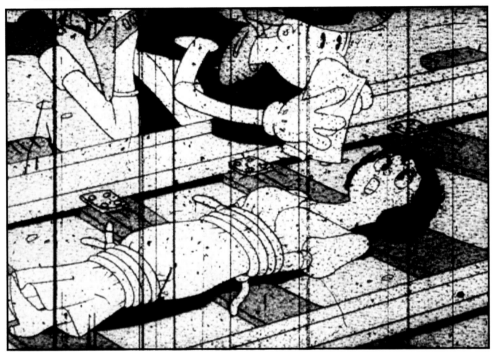

Everything that comes out of their mouth is pre-programmed tripe: 'Thank you, come again'; 'Did you find everything you were looking for?'; 'How are you?' The last one bothers me the most. Why do we ask a question when we don't care about the answer? Shall I really tell you how my day has been? Of course not, cause no one cares. You're expected to say 'good,' 'fine,' 'not bad.'

"How could you let this happen?", I ask

"I did not let this happen. I have given you free will. If I played humans like puppets, how is that different from getting all you want from vending machines?"

Silence.

Even God has no answer.

Dizziness.

Everything around me is distorted. I feel like I'm in the frame of
a film. I see sky above, sky below. They flicker and change.
Come together, fall apart. A cowboy rides on a cloud. Confusion.

"Th
en
it's   allllllllllllllllllllll
ran
dom.

I   t
's   all
lu   ck.

We
're
in
Ve
gas   every

                                              mom
ent   of
our
lives."

Finally. It stops. I collect my senses.
"I could use a drop of water."

We jump into the ocean.
Nearby, a man sits on a raft.
"May we have some water?"
"There is water all around you."
"I don't like sea water."

Tezuka interrupts and says, "Look, do you see that?"

61

"What?"

"A mermaid."

"You're nuts. I see a fish."

"You can't see the mermaid?"

"There's no such thing."

"If I see it, it must be."

"You should get help. Take a rest. Maybe you're stressed out. It's not good to have such a vivid imagination. They could lock you up."

Annoyed, Tezuka bids me farewell and dives into the water.

He vanishes under the waves as I cling to the raft.

Then, with the grace of dancers, two fish leap into the air before falling back to whence they came.

Continuing to drift, I see a pirate ship. For a second, I think I see my late grandfather at the helm of the boat. He drinks from a bottle and howls. I call out, but he doesn't hear me. The ship sails on.

The raft eventually drifts to the shore.

An older male puppet greets me.

"Hello, I've been expecting you. My name is **Tadanari Okamoto**. There is more than what you have seen. You have seen much darkness, but there is light to be found if you open your eyes and heart."

I feel myself transform into a boy again.

"I'm scared. People keep leaving. Why is there so much pain?"

"Look at these two hunters. Both have demons. The one who fights demons and illnesses suffers. The one who befriends his demon and accepts the small ills of existence will lead a peaceful, honourable life. The other will suffer."

Figure 48.
*Restaurant of
Many Orders.*

Okamoto shows me more visions, innocent worlds under threat. Villains stealing formulas, money and creating havoc in a city. Aliens invade a peaceful, harmonious children's amusement park. The innocent, wondrous love and imagination of a young boy are shattered by the death of the girl he loves.

"What kind of world is this? Look at this monkey and crab. The monkey murders the crab. His children are born from his death and spend their time seeking revenge on the monkey. Is that living with your demons? Accepting the ills of existence?"

"It is the price of freedom and possibility. Anything is possible, including violence, sadness, loneliness and death. This is the price of possibility."

"But it is scary. I want certainty. I want to know that I will live a long life, that I will see my children become men."

63

"It's not possible. You must live now. You must overcome these fears and embrace the moments that you have. Life is a series of moments that you create and define. You must live in the present, not the past, not the future."

He fades away. No more. Just me.

Okamoto was a pretty impressive fella, the renaissance man of Japanese animation. Like Prince, Okamoto can play all the instruments. He animates with puppets, wood, yarn, clay, pencil, marker, cel, plastic. He made educational films, public service announcements, commercials, TV shows, music videos and short films. His short films – made for children and adults – use folk tales and modern stories to convey the complexities of the human soul.

Most of you probably haven't heard of Tadanari Okamoto. I know him solely because of his final film, *Restaurant of Many Orders* (1991). It was played at the Ottawa '92 animation festival and it left a strong impression on me.

What amazes me is that despite an impressive body of work (both quality and quantity), Okamoto is not as well known internationally as Kawamoto, Kuri and Tezuka. Rich in content and technique, many of Okamoto's works stand tall beside any of the international animation "classics". So why the heck isn't he more known? Might be due to language. His films are loaded with dialogue and narration. Even with subtitles, you'd be hard pressed to fully comprehend the nuances of Okamoto's deeply Japanese films.

Imagine my frustration having access to four of DVDs containing pretty much all of Okamoto's work – without English subtitles. But what can you do without a live-in Japanese translator? Fortunately, a couple of fine fellows (Nobuaki Doi and Ben Enringer) helped me figure out the storylines that I couldn't piece together myself.

Like so many animators, Okamoto didn't intend on becoming an animator. He actually studied as a lawyer and then gave it up to get into film. "I wanted to work in the movies. But I wanted to do something where the art side would be the major element.

So I wound up in animation. But when I arrived, what people called 'animation' seemed far removed from my own notion of art."

Okamoto's early films certainly reflect his concerns about animation. *A Wonderful Medicine (1965), Welcome, Alien (1966),* and *Operation Woodpecker (1966)* are all solid, entertaining films with some beautiful character and background designs, but conceptual they are nothing special.

His first important film – at least in my books – is *Chikotan* (1971). What begins as a charming story about a young boy who has a crush on his classmate, Chikotan. They make a promise to marry when they grow up, but this beautiful moment of innocence is destroyed when Chikotan dies in a car accident. It's a shocking, tragic ending that takes the viewer completely by surprise. The twist shows Okamoto's devilish side, luring the viewer into what seems like a sweet little children's film and then punching us in the gut.

Chikotan is also the first film where Okamoto ditches puppets for cel animation. His use of crayon drawings is an apt reflection of childhood and a perfect tool for capturing the frantic blur of childhood and with it, life and death.

During the 1970s, Okamoto made at least 23 films (not including commercials). This is an astonishing amount of productivity – especially for an artist whose work is so diverse and intricate.

"If I've focused obsessively on new stylistic methods and approaches to sound all these years, it wasn't out of some desire to show off or prove that I'm the best, but to be true to my personal vision. I always believed in the unlimited expressive potential of animation, ever since I started working in animation. That's why I never allowed myself to use the same style or method twice in a row in my films, but instead always forced myself to look for new expressive means."

Of course, not all of the films are memorable. Okamoto's tendency to make longer films sometimes makes for a fairly tedious viewing experience – even though the works are always technically innovative. Even Okamoto admitted in 1986 that "it's been a continuous process of trial and error that has resulted in major losses in terms of both time and money, but that has also made it possible for me to discover a tailor-made production style that enables me to circumvent a major chunk of the technical drudgery inherent in the animation production process. If I've been able to produce more than 30 films, both short and long, over the last 20 years (entirely apart from commissioned work), it's largely thanks to my rational simplification of the production process."

With utmost ease, Okamoto frequently jumped between folk tales, modern cautionary stories and children's stories. His stories set in the past are often based on traditional forms of Japanese storytelling.

The marvelous *Mochimochi Tree* (1972) uses paper/collage and a gidayu narrative, a form of singing narration performed by a chanter (gidayu comes from ancient bunraku, a traditional puppet, plays) to tell a story about a young boy who lives with his grandfather. The boy is petrified of the dark so his grandfather tells him he should see the Mochimochi tree, which lights up in the middle of the night. On the night they are to visit the tree, the grandfather becomes sick. Frantic, the boy races through dark, cold paths to find a doctor. On his way back with the doctor, the boy sees the Mochimochi tree. In the haze of the moment, the boy's obvious love of his grandfather helps him overcome his fears. In blunt terms, when the ???? hits the fan the boy shows that he's got the moxie to put his fears aside and help someone in need. A trait so many of us lack.

Praise Be To Small Ills (1973) is another Okamoto masterpiece. A song is sung to a sick young girl. The song sings of two hunters: a weak hunter with a blue demon and the stronger hunter with the red demon. The weak hunter ends up the stronger of the two. He goes with the flow of life, accepting and overcoming life's set backs (i.e. demons/ills). He leaves life peacefully. On the other hand, the strong hunter, overconfident about his strength, perhaps feeling somewhat indestructible, dies a tragic death.

Again, Okamoto addresses the fragility of life through this sombre tale of love, death, joys and ills. Life is too short to let your demons get the best of you. The road will be a lot smoother if you just accept them as a part of life, realizing to that there is always someone else with bigger demons.

Technically, *Praise Be To Small Ills*, is another work of inspired innovation that draws on Japanese traditions. Inspired by ema, small wooden plaques that hang in a shrine (on the plaques Shinto worshipers write their prayers and desires to the gods), Okamoto uses cedar planks combined with raw drawings.

Community, strength and sacrifice are common themes throughout Okamoto's career. People who make sacrifices for the benefit of others will be rewarded in Okamoto's world.

Strong Bridge (1976), based on a ghost story by Yakumo Koizumi, tells the story of a man walking through the woods. A ghost woman with a baby stands at the foot of a bridge. She approaches him, gives him the ghost baby and disappears across the bridge. Freaked out, the man crosses the bridge to give the baby back to the woman. However, midway across, the bridge begins shaking. The baby becomes heavier, but the man endures the weight and crosses the bridge. The baby disappears. It turns out the man has helped give life to the ghost baby. As a reward the man is given strength by the gods.

In *Towards the Rainbow* (1977) two villages are separated by a river. When a man and woman from each side, fall in love with each other, the villagers – in a beautiful gesture – join together to build a bridge so that the lovers can come together. Okamoto uses a mix of puppet animation, including some incredibly rich and detailed rocky landscapes, and what seems to be drawn animation to capture the rough waves of the water. Okamoto even adds animated mist to evoke a greater sense of realism.

In *The Soba Flower of Mount Oni* (1979) – which uses an odd combination of watercolours on cels – a demon terrorizes a village in search of soba (buckwheat noodles). With the help of a young girl, the demon learns to make his own soba. Realizing how terrible his actions have been, the demon makes peace with the villagers. When the village is threatened by flooding, the demon makes the ultimate sacrifice by turning himself into a rock to save the people.

The Magic Ballad (1982) is one of Okamoto's most touching and tragic films about strength, sacrifice and mortality. An ailing old

Itako (psychic) woman who used to attack the ghosts of foxes (Japanese thought that foxes had magical powers) is visited by a fox. It turns out the fox has special healing powers when he sings a certain song. The duo become friends and travel the countryside healing the sick. Tragedy strikes when the old lady is attacked by a robber. The fox steps in to save the woman and is fatally wounded. In the heartbreaking finale, the woman attempts to sing the fox back to life, but fails because her singing is terrible.

Along with *Chikotan, The Magic Ballad* is one of Okamoto's most touching and heart wrenching works. The final scene is masterpiece of dramatic power that shows how effective puppets can be in capturing and conveying the deepest, darkest emotions of the human soul.

Traditional tales were not Okamoto's only sources. He also made more modern-orientated films that address various social problems of contemporary Japanese society. While none of the films are particularly special, it is interesting to see how very different Okamoto's perspective is on modern society. The films are far more cynical, revealing mild contempt toward the state of the world. In *The Travelling Companion*, (1973), Okamato addresses the problem of drunk driving. The *Phone Booth*, (1975), deals with the impatience, selfishness and the general anti-social behaviour of a woman hogging the phone while a man waits and waits to use it. *Shhh!*, (1980), uses fast-paced, breathless narration, to lament the loss of a quiet, calm, unpolluted world that has been replaced by an endless assault of noise.

Okamoto died in 1991 and his final film, *The Restaurant of Many Orders* (1991) was completed by Kihachiro Kawamoto. In this film, Okamoto attacks the frivolousness of a society that kills animals for pleasure. Based on a story by the famous Japanese writer, Kenji Miyazawa, and in the vein of *Battle Royale* and *The Most Dangerous Game*, *The Restaurant of Many Orders* is about hunters who become the hunted.

Two hunters, lost in the woods, find a restaurant. They enter and find no one around. Inside the men find different rooms. Inside there are orders (e.g. "leave your guns here".) Thinking they're in for a wonderful meal, the two men continue to search for the dining room. The finally enter a large barren room. A table sits in the middle of the room. A cook pours two glasses of wine and invites them to take a seat. Water drips. Three lovely Louise Brooks lookalikes enter and perform a sensual dance for the men. It's all going good. ... until the women turn into wild black cats and attack the men. It turns out that they are the meal. The men finally escape and hitch a ride back to town. The horror is over.

The ending of the film is unsatisfactory. It's not clear how the men escaped, nor what they learned from their violent encounter. Visually, the film is another innovative success for Okamoto. Using copper-coloured drawings that bring to mind the work of Polish animator Piotr Dumala, Okamoto creates a claustrophobic Kafka-esque nightmare.

69

Interestingly, Okamoto had strong views about the animation world. He was very critical about mass-produced animation that rejected the individuality of personal animation "in favour of conformity and accessibility".

Okamoto believed that personal animation might eventually "become unfeasible for lack of funding". He was wrong though. Okamoto seemed to believe that "giant conglomerates (would) enter the picture ... making it harder for small-scale individual animation to survive". He failed to realize that technology had the opposite effect, creating a more affordable and visible medium that offered more opportunities for independent animators and smaller "boutique" studios.

It's a shame Okamoto didn't live to see animation flourish and grow.

Okamoto's faith in the idea that good deeds will bring harmony and rewards is admirable, but idealistic. Sadly, I fear the world is far more complex – if we assume there is no higher power guiding us, then we are free to do as we please? Are good and bad merely guidelines created by humanity? As such, the bad are not always punished, while the good do not always find the rainbow. Is there a rainbow?

Assailed by these thoughts I hear Okamoto's reassuring voice: "How else could I possibly go on doing something as hard as animation without a dream to hold on to?"

Hold on. So I do.

I'm now on dry land. An island. A figure appears and offers me a hand to hold. It's not a human hand. Feels like wood. The body catches up. It's a strange looking puppet human hybrid – a short Japanese puppet guy with glasses. I jump back, startled. I don't like puppets. They freak me out. When I was very young, I remember walking a street in Toronto with my grandmother. A girl passed the other way carrying a Raggedy Ann doll. Thing spooked me. Couldn't sleep. Couldn't get that strange living dead image out of my head. And that's the thing, that eerie fusion of life and death. A figure so fragile and human, yet not.

"Don't be afraid", says the puppet. "I am **Kihachiro Kawamoto**. I know you have endured great pain recently. I understand this, but suffering is inevitable."

He knows of what he speaks. Like most Japanese of his generation he has witnessed war. "I was a second lieutenant when the bombing of Tokyo in World War II happened on March 10th, 1945. Because I was in a construction site in the suburb of Tokyo, I didn't suffer from the bombing directly, but I saw the burning red sky on the city of Tokyo. During the war, I stayed in Japan and never went to the front because the number of planes and ships in Japan were very limited at the end of the war. But there is no doubt that the biggest suffering in life is war."

Kawamoto tells me about Buddhism and how there are four basic sufferings in a person's life: birth, disease, aging, dying.

"There are many types of Suffering: Sei-Byou-Rou-Shi (suffering from living, disease, getting old and death), Ai-Betsu-Ri-Ku (suffering from parting from someone you love), On-Zoh-E-Ku (suffering from meeting with people you hate), Gu-Fu-Toku-Fu (suffering from not getting what you want), Go-Un-Jyou-Ku (suffering from the all things of the universe.)"

In order to overcome these sufferings, he tells me, we must achieve a state of "Satori", a state of enlightenment. A kick in the ass, in a sense.

"But how does one get to Satori?"

"Buddha answers that it comes from the feeling of Syushin, when one desires or seeks to capture what you can never get."

We walk and stop by a cherry tree. Nearby we see a monk passing with his young assistant. "Sit down", says Kawamoto. "Let's watch." Confused, I assent.

The monk asks the young man to guard the cherry tree so that no one breaks any branches. A bit of a lush, the young man

allows a couple of guys to get past the gate and near the tree. They get him liquored up. He passes out. The men run off with a branch. The monk returns, pissed to discover the branch missing. Chases the young man around.

"That's pretty funny."

The light fades.

"Form is emptiness and emptiness is form."

A creepy old woman lies on a bed. She's dying. Her sons tell her they are going hunting. We follow them in the forest. Something is not right. It's very creepy. Sights and sounds mystify. Suddenly, a hand reaches out from a tree and grabs one of the guys by the hair. Freaked out, he screams. His brother fires an

Figure 50. *The Breaking of Branches is Forbidden.*

Figure 51. *The Demony.*

Figure 52. *The Dojoji Temple.*

arrow severing the hand from the unseen body. The brothers return home to find their mother crawling on the ground minus a hand. She transforms into a demon and floats off.

Figure 53. *Briar Rose or Sleeping Beauty.*

The woman has suffered a hard life. Negligent parents.

Unloving husband. Illness. A broken, miserable existence.

Old people get angry as their age and eat their children?

Kawamoto shows me more suffering women. A crazy woman falls for a Buddhist monk and stalks him across the land as he heads to a temple. She turns into a serpent during the chase. This is basically *Fatal Attraction*. The monk sacrifices himself to take the venom out of the woman. Beaten, humiliated, scorned she plunges into the river.

A mother never stops longing for old lover. Later, her daughter falls for the guy too. She makes love to him. While they're getting busy, the classy guy whispers her mother's name. A spindle (phallic symbol, anyone) spins. The man disappears. The daughter finds herself in the same boat as her mother. Making due with a husband she doesn't love. A life of compromise. Can't always get what you want.

Figure 54. *The House of Flames.*

Another woman CAN get what she wants. Two guys are hot for her. She can't decide. Rather than cause one of them grief, she kills herself. In their grief, the men kill each other. The trio of madness meet in hell. The guys burn the woman.

I feel like I'm watching soap operas or 1950s Hollywood melodramas. Love makes people nuts. They become obsessive and selfish.

"Mr. Kawamoto. How come all your women are nuts? And why is love so horrid? Is love not the key to harmony and happiness?

"What women do in my films is the result of their 'Syushin.' They don't intend to make their family and they are not crazy."

We walk on.

More suffering. Dogs race by. People applaud. They are not puppets now, but cut outs. Colour fades to black and white. Lights fade. Announcer calls the race. We see nothing. Starter interrupts and asks the audience to see the truth, that the dogs are tearing each other apart. They are being deceived, their tickets are no different than the plastic fish that tempt the dogs. A shot rings out. Starter falls. People turn to dogs. Blood red rose grows next to man's body.

The same theme, but a stranger film, more politicized, dealing with a manipulative and deceptive state (aka. Communist countries of the time, like Czechoslovakia).

I remember that Kawamoto loves the films of Czech puppet master, Jiri Trnka.

"When I first saw Trnka's *The Emperor's Nightingale* the film shocked me so deeply that I couldn't stand up for a while. From that moment, Czech became the country where I should visit someday."

Kawamoto's desire came true. He went to Czechoslovakia and met Trnka. "He told me the essence of puppet and this is really important for me. What he said was such things: 'Puppet is never a miniature of human.' 'Puppets have their own world.' "

"He told me that I must study Japanese stylized plays, such as Noh or Bunraku, to make my films. These words from him became the basis of my animation."

"What are these types of plays? I've heard the name 'Noh,' but I have no idea what it means."

"Noh is a traditional Japanese play. Bunraku is a puppet play from the Edo period. Both deal primarily with Syushin. There are many highlights in Bunraku such as 'Syura' (battles), 'Chari' (comical movements), 'Daijyo' (solemn opening), but what is the most important for expressions of puppets there is 'Syuutan' (sorrow). There is no doubt that one of the most important

moments in Bunraku play is 'Kudoki', where a woman protagonist (of course puppet) tells about her suffering. Bunraku directors knew that the viewer got a stronger impression by using puppets than by using actors."

Figure 55. *The Travel*

Kawamoto suddenly freaks out. Is he having a seizure? He turns into clay and starts to create a woman. The woman turns into a devil. The devil and Kawamoto battle. It goes on and on and on. They fight to no conclusion.

Black.

Airport. Puppet Kawamoto returns. "We're going on a trip with this young woman." We fly to an unknown place. There we encounter an assortment of strange objects and people including a blind man who jumps to his death, a creepy short blue man who eats body parts he grabs from inside a heart. We walk down a street littered with mementos of history, along with a litany of reminders that the world can be cruel, chaotic and apathetic.

A man meditates, then combusts. We sit by the sea. Calm. At peace. The meditative man appears in the sky and comforts us, but then vanishes.

Nothing is permanent in this world of pain and suffering. Death is a release?

The Book of the Dead, (2005), Kawamoto's latest film, is the most hopeful of all his work. All the themes of his earlier films are here. In fact, like Bergman's *Fanny and Alexander*, *The Book of the Dead* feels like a summary of Kawamoto's career.

Figure 56. *The Book of the Dead*

Set in the Nara period (710-784 or thereabouts), not long after Buddhism arrived in Japan, *The Book of the Dead* follows Iratsume, the devout and noble daughter of the second house of the Fujiwara clan, who has taken upon herself the rather futile task of transcribing 1,000 copies of the *Amida Sutra*. After working endlessly for a year, the exhausted woman has a vision of the Buddha shining over the holy mountain Futakami. Hypnotized she sets out for a sacred temple.

Along the way, Iratsume meets the ghost of Prince Otsu. He believes that Iratsume is the young woman whose beautiful face was the last thing Otsu saw before he died. Otsu is haunted by the face and he becomes obsessed with Iratsume and the world of the living.

Iratsume, who has turned her back on the material world as she searches for the spiritual, mistakenly believes that Otsu's flesh might be a manifestation of the Buddha. She makes a shroud for Otsu that is covered with Buddhist imagery. The shroud becomes a mandala (a symbolic representation of attaining oneness) and saves Otsu's soul and unifies her with Buddha.

If it turns out to be Kawamoto's final film, it's a fitting end to his career and life. *The Book of the Dead* is his gift to future generations and a warning about become too attached to either the divine or material worlds. Kawamoto's work suggests that we cherish the moment and not worry about the future or carry forward the baggage of the past. There's no point to it. We go from nothing to nothing. Why stress out over things that cannot be controlled, that do not matter in the end?

I wake up on an empty road. Kawamoto has gone.

Something has happened to me, but I'm not sure what.

I turn my sights to Tokyo.

Akihabara.

After wandering through endless cramped and crammed electronic, anime and otaku shops, I grab a seat in a maid café. Young girls are dressed in sexy (are there any other kind?) maid outfits. They speak in squeaky subservient voices. Place is littered with otaku, their fat bodies exhausted from a day of shopping for anime and girlfriend pillows. Yes, girlfriend pillows. I remember reading a story about a freak geek in love with his pillow. Whatever works I guess. But I wonder, does the pillow love back?

Outside, Halloween is everywhere, all the time. Street musicians do weak impressions of American rock. One sings an old Jam song, *This is the Modern World*, a '70s pulsating punk song of fierce rebellion and frustration with a stifling British society and an apathetic burned-out post-Vietnam culture.

I take a sip from my coffee and look around. Is this the modern world? Is that what previous generations fought for? Are these the lessons of Hiroshima? I don't know. I don't judge. I just wonder.

As I wonder I see a familiar figure walking. **Yoji Kuri**. Famous guy. The timing is fitting.

Kuri's animation films have that same bite, lifting Japanese animation – Tezuka aside – out of decades of cozy narrative cartoons into a new era of graphic and conceptual experimentation. His films mock and shock by attacking technology, population expansion, monotony of modern society while playfully toiling with the tricky goings-on between guys and gals.

Witnessing the surrender of Japan during the Second World War, the devastation of his country followed by the quick rise of Western inspired materialist culture and rampant consumption, Kuri, like many of his colleagues of the time, questioned the state and direction of his society and world.

In one of his first films, *Two Pikes* (1961), Kuri blasts modernization and endless expansion of Tokyo (and other major modern cities). A man and woman adrift at sea land on an island. They build a home and settle into a comfortable, peaceful hardworking routine. One day a man arrives. He brings a machine. The machine makes work easier, giving the couple more leisure time. Soon more people arrive on the island and a cascade of buildings spring up to the skies. The island is now cramped and polluted. Eventually, war brings an end to the island and the couple is left alone, stranded again.

In *A Man Next Door (1965)*, a red-hatted man is unable to sleep because of the constant racket of his neighbour – who types, drinks, walks the walls (literally), jams with a band, builds a rocket. Fed up, the red man moves his house to a quieter spot. After a moment of silence, a noise assault invades his room. He's now surrounded by many noisy neighbours. Tokyo is criticized for overcrowding, cramped conditions, but Kuri always cautions us that things can always get worse.

Later in the McLaren-inspired *The Chair* (1964), Kuri films a number of different people from varying backgrounds sitting on

Figure 57. *Two Pikes*

a chair. The people have been asked to sit for 15 minutes. They sit, read, smoke, dance, strip, sleep etc. ... Familiar gestures and movements are sped up, twisted into strange, mechanical movements. A choreography of the mundane. People, Kuri says, do not know how to do nothing. They must always be busy, always moving, doing something. Is this bad or is it a question about where this frenzied existence is going?

Cynicism floods Kuri's films. His characters are no good for the most part. In *The Room* (1967), we see the life of an apartment

Figure 58.
Human Zoo.

through the lights of the windows. Fires, adultery, robbery and madmen engulf the building. *Au Fou!*, (1968), a tedious string of gags about killing, touches upon Japan's notorious reputation as a country of suicides.

Koji's characters, like the inhabitants of Tokyo, live and move in suffocating, claustrophobic spaces of coldness and misery. Despite the close proximity, intimacy is non-existent. People just want privacy and solitude to live out their tedious lives.

Like Kawamoto's works, love offers no hope in Kuri's world. Kuri pushes aside romantic myths of love and marriage to reveal the violence, obsession, suffocation, and annoyance behind the facade. In *Human Zoo*, (1962), the film that put Kuri on the world animation map, a man and woman are locked in a cage. The woman beats, sits on, pokes and collars the clucking, grunting, peeping man. *Love*, (1963), a virtual sequel, extends the riff. This time a woman chases a man all over the place. She captures him, eats him and then excretes him out. He flees. She pursues. So it goes.

Kuri also dabbles in experimental, seemingly stream of consciousness works (*Tragedy of the G-Line (1969)*, *AOS*, (1964), *The Midnight Parasites* (1972) that, again, contain the familiar

Figure 59. *Love*

themes of gender struggles, violence, boredom, and body parts (a reoccurring image in his films).

Working with a vocal composition by Yoko Ono, Kuri took the avant-garde artist's assorted screams, moans, licks, and grunts and twisted them into a surreal series of black and white scenarios often involving discombobulated body parts of men and women who exist in cramped, isolated trappings unable to connect, touch the other.

The Midnight Parasites is a dark, cynical piece that takes place in a barren landscape. The environment is littered with bizarre

Figure 60. *AOS*

creatures that repeatedly kill and eat one another. Surrealism and absurdity aside, Kuri portrays a world that, in his mind, has gone to waste.

As his career moves forward, Kuri's cynicism and obsession with the same themes becomes increasingly repetitive and tedious. Yes, society is garbage. Yes, men and women treat each other like garbage. Is that it? Is that all he has to say? Kuri offers no hope for this world, no solutions, suggestions or alternatives. It's a lazy cop-out in the end.

Still, Kuri's importance on the Japanese animation circuit cannot be understated. He's among the first Japanese animators to move away from the obvious Disney influence toward a style that has more in common with James Thurber, Saul Steinberg and the Zagreb animation. His minimalist, experimental style marks a shift from the polished beauty and innocence of earlier Japanese works toward a more challenging, surreal work that routinely criticizes Japanese society and world politics.

The maid arrives with my coffee. Took her 20 minutes to bring me a coffee. I tell her that she's been a bad girl.

"I should be punished", she teases. She then hands me a wood paddle and pulls up her dress.

"Spank me, Master."

I'm a bit freaked out. I remember the time I met a woman through the personal ads. We went out and ended up back at my place. While we kissed she told me to, in no specific order, bite her, smack her and pull her hair. After a few half-hearted tugs on her hair I told her it was time to leave.

But, heck, when in Rome ... I take the paddle and smack the maid's panty-covered rump. After each THWACK she lets out a sexy, mousey squeak. Done, she says thank you and comes back with the bill.

I get charged for the spanking.

Hiroshima

Flying to Hiroshima, I can't stop thinking about IT. Sad really. A city that is almost entirely known for one of the most devastating events in human history. How odd that it has become a source of income today, a grotesque tourist destination. I admit it. It's why I came here. Sure there's an animation festival here, but Sayoko Kinoshita, the festival's director, is in Tokyo. There's no real reason for me to be here, but I had to come, had to see it.

As we fly toward the city, I feel nervous and nauseous. I imagine the bombers flying over Hiroshima. What was going through the minds of the men onboard the *Enola Gay*? "My god, what have we done?" said the co-pilot. The pilot said he never had regrets. "We saved lives", he mused. I dunno. Did they? Maybe. Maybe they ended the war earlier and prevented thousands more deaths, but how many of those deaths would have been, shall we say, innocent? The life of a soldier is no less than that of a civilian, but they are there to do a job. Death is a very real part of that job. Was it a part of the job for the women and children of Hiroshima who were incinerated in the bombing? Then again, Japan was no victim, committing horrific atrocities throughout China before and during The Second World War.

In the end, I can't help but think of the many innocent men, women and children slaughtered before, during and after the war because of the petty fights and greed of others.

I try to reconcile my brother's death. How can I drown in grief knowing the suffering others have endured? One death. One person. It can't compare to the thousands upon thousands killed here. I know that, but it doesn't make me feel any better. I can only know what I experience. This death hurts more than anything I've ever experienced and deep down it really doesn't matter at this moment that there are people worse off than me.

As we approach the Hiroshima airport, I see images of Renzo and Sayoko Kinoshita's film, *Pica Don* (1978). It was the first animation film made about the Hiroshima bombing. Pica describes the flash of the A-bomb, apparently infinitely brighter than the sun. Don is the shock wave that follows the flash.

Figure 61. *Pica Don.*

It's a blue sky, hardly a cloud. A family gets ready for their day. A young boy plays. His older sister is dressed and ready for school. Father prepares for work. As they head to their destinations, the inhabitants of Hiroshima also go about their business. It's just another day, no more special or worse than any other. Birds soar. People walk. A mother breast feeds her baby.

The tension builds. It's far too quiet. A clock ticks.

Planes fly overhead and catch the attention of young boys.

Nothing.

Air sirens.

Another plane.

Something falls from it.

A blinding flash.

A sound wave tears through people. Instant incineration.

In, literally, a flash, a heavenly day becomes a torched landscape of hell. Bodies melt. Grotesque forms are indistinguishable from the rubble around them.

The happy family is no more. The final image rests on the remains of the young boy.

Makes me sick to think of the film again. First time I saw it was in Italy. My son, Jarvis, then 7, was with my wife and I. The Italians decided to screen *Pica Don* before their closing ceremonies. Nice way to set the mood.

I've watched documentaries from both American and Japanese perspectives. Each side has their justification. The Japanese say it was not an act of war, but the mass slaughter of civilians. The Americans say that it was the only way to put an end to the war and save more lives. The Kinoshitas don't care who is to blame. It's not the cause, but the effect. Innocent human lives were decimated. It's as simple and horrific as that.

Pica Don, like all of the Kinoshitas' films, is a documentary. For *Pica Don*, the duo spent years researching the Hiroshima bombing, sifting through books, documents, photos and drawings, and interviewing many survivors.

Sayoko told me that she constructed "scenarios and stories by weaving the facts and realities. Those scenes like hands pulled off, and eyes coming out ... were experienced by so many victims."

Surprisingly – or perhaps not given the general perception that animation is a facile entertainment vehicle – many survivors were pissed that the tragedy was being shown using animation.

"At that time in Japan", Sayoko told me, "animation (manga) was known as TV series for children. So, most survivors felt (were even angry) that we were not serious. However, when the film was completed and shown, people of Japan and especially the local people of Hiroshima, appreciated us very much for

Figure 62. The Last Air Raid: Kumagaya.

making this film. Also, every TV news, radios, newspapers and magazines focused on *Pica Don* immediately, and it was shown in the schools all over Japan. Also, it is shown freely and permanently at the Peace Memorial Museum in Hiroshima."

Using a more straightforward narrative and a naturalistic design with anime characteristics (e.g. the big disgustingly cute eyes), *The Last Air Raid: Kumagaya* (1993) continues the exploration of the devastating effects of war on innocent people, specifically children. Sachiko, a seven-year-old girl who has lost her entire family in a bombing in Tokyo heads to Kumagaya to live with her uncle's family. One day later, the city is bombed and the girl

– and many others – dies. Most of the houses in Kumagaya were made of wood so the entire city was destroyed by the bombs.

Figure 63. *Made in Okinawa*

And for what purpose?

Japan had clearly lost the war by this point. Why was an air raid ordered?

Hours after the bombing, the Japanese surrendered.

Last Air Raid goes beyond blaming the allies and also targets the Japanese government and military. "People were brainwashed and excited that Japanese military was gaining great victories at Asian countries", says Sayoko. "However, it meant nothing but atrocities. Just like any other war (even today), people are always controlled by the government. ... Most Japanese people were not aware of the deception of their government and military, but rather believed in their government."

Made in Okinawa (2004), the third of their anti-war films, explores the sweeping changes made in Japan's southern island, a frequent target of invasion because of its strategic importance for invaders. As a man lies on a beach watching the calm seas, history sails by him bringing war, occupation, invasion (Okinawa was the only place where land battles occurred during the Second World War), and industrial change. For once, the Kinoshitas offer a whisper of hope. Despite the massive changes in Okinawa's history, the man remains on the beach, calmly watching the sea. History changes, but the essence of the people and culture remains.

Figure 64. *What on Earth is He?*.

All three animation documentaries avoid taking sides. "We wanted to describe 'war is just killing between people,' which is only merciless, tragic and really hopeless, and that we should not make war", Sayoko notes. "Renzo and I wanted to make these films in order to pass the story to our future generation. As human beings are not very clever, we really have to study from our past faults."

Idealized existence is a common hope throughout the Kinoshita's work. *In What on Earth Is He?* (1971) *and A Little Journey* (1994), they criticize the pollution problems of Japan.

Figure 65. *Made in Japan*

What on Earth is He? is a bizarre little film about people's nose hairs growing longer and longer to the point where they struggle to breathe. Not having any clue what the nose hair thread was about I asked Sayoko. "There was a rumour at that time, half joking and laughing, that human beings try to protect themselves and survive from air pollution, and thus, nose hairs will be very long. However, the reality was very severe, and no one could really laugh. Many, many people suffered with asthma, but the government control was very weak, and factories did not care at all about environment."

In *A Little Journey*, a naked little kid and his cat live harmoniously in the country until construction trucks arrive and decimate the land. In search of his lost cat, the boy heads to the city and is overwhelmed by noise and pollution. With nowhere to turn the boy and – now found – cat fly beyond the Earth in search of something better.

In *Made in Japan* (1972), the commercialization of Japanese traditions is satirized. Japan, in their eyes, has become an exotic tourist shop. In *Japonese*, (1977), a sort of follow up to *Made in Japan*, the Kinoshitas turn their satirical eyes toward Western culture and how it's infiltrated and dumbed down Japanese

Figure 66.
Japonese.

society. Using a combination of drawings, collage and cut-out images, the film begins (as many of their films do) with a scene of stillness, a Japanese man enjoying a calm and serene existence only to have it invaded by the noise and clutter of modern society.

While I sense a hard criticism about the changes in Japanese society, Sayoko denies this.

"We try to depict and describe the situation and even ourselves objectively." Yet, at the same time, Sayoko adds that "we wanted to give a warning to the growing commercialism and capitalism of Japan at that time, and which continues today.

In the old days, Japan had its own important philosophy based more on Zen – human beings are born as nothing, and die as nothing, but still, human beings struggle in order to enhance their philosophical stage. Also, as an agricultural people, we felt profound reverence for nature. Through Japan's modernization though, people became more flooded by materialism, and were apt to lose their identity."

Despite Sayoko's words, both films are critical and clearly take a stance on what they perceive as dour changes effecting Japanese society.

The Kinoshita's films routinely begin in a state of calmness. Individuals are seen enjoying a solitary, serene existence, in touch with the landscape around them. Very quickly that harmonious existence is threatened and ultimately destroyed by history, by war, invasion and modernization. More than any of the other Japanese animators, the Kinoshitas are passionate about the preservation of their history and culture. If globalization cannot be stopped, indigenous culture and history can at least be breathed forward and not forgotten.

What I don't quite understand is how after their concerns and their criticism of aspects of modern Japanese society, the Kinoshitas don't mind making a slew of animation commercials that promote the very materialist culture they abhor and protest. That said, they did pour their own money into their indie films. Working on commercials and TV jobs helped them earn money to continue making their own films.

Admittedly, the ads show their diversity as animators while adding to the myths about the oddity of Japanese commercials. My personal favourite is a commercial for what I think is salt … or something similar. The ad is a lavish production of animation, a swinging '60s tune à la Burt Bacharach, and, get this, a gaggle of dancers. It's like *Laugh In* compressed to a minute.

I would like to buy into the Kinoshitas genuine plea for peace, but the cynical side of me looks back at the history of mankind and sees a litany of war and violence. It's the way of the world and a few socially conscious animation films aren't going to do anything about it. Cynical? Apathetic? No, just realistic about the nature of humanity. The films are touching, heartwarming and honest, but I guess I've become far too cynical to buy into their desire for a teddy bear world of harmony and happiness. Of course, what right do I have to be cynical? My life has been void of war, 9/11 being the closest thing. Until Barry's death, I had only suffered one other death of a relative. Relatively speaking, I've had a pretty harmonious and happy life. Yet I remain

Figure 67.
Toshiba Tinitron.

fiercely cynical. Why? Cowardice? A fear that giving over to joy would be futile because my life will one day be taken, just as my brother's was?

Losing a brother, one person, seems to pale in comparison to what the people of Japan (and other countries) have endured. They have lost all their relatives, neighbours, colleagues in a flash. For what purpose? For what reason? There is no answer.

After arriving in Hiroshima, I head to Miyajima Island, the Island of the Gods. It's just outside Hiroshima. I take the ferry across the island and pass the red Otorii gates, which stand 16 metres tall.

Tourists, like me, aside, it's a beautiful, serene landscape. Mountains surround the island. Deer roam freely. I walk around the Itsushima Shrine and encounter various shrines, statues and temples.

Calmness. I feel at ease here, outside the haze of my journey, the numbing dreamscape of my grief. Everything seems so far away. All the minute problems and challenges vanish. Barry would have loved this island. Easily excitable, he'd be racing around, exploring the place, freely asking questions to anyone working here. Unlike me, he never shied away. He was intellectually aggressive in a jovial, genuine and unpretentious manner. Always a boy, he was curious about everything the world had to offer.

A brief smile passes.

Reluctantly, I leave the island and head back to Hiroshima. Entering the city, the urban assault begins again.

After chowing down the Hiroshima specialty, okonomiyaki (looks a bit like a pancake, but is stuffed with egg, meat and whatever else you want. Good hangover food), I figure it's time to check the Hiroshima Peace Memorial Museum. I'm nervous about going. I don't know why. I've felt uncomfortable the entire time I've been in the city. It's ludicrous, but walking through the city has been unnerving. I feel claustrophobic, wondering where I'd scurry if the city was attacked.

Walking from the museum, I walk to the only building left standing after bombing. It's haunting. I get chills standing near it. It's fairly non-descript. Looks like any government-style structure. The first part of the exhibit focuses on the general history of the atomic bomb, the bombing of Hiroshima and the beginning of the nuclear age. This section concentrates on information and facts about the dangers of nuclear weapons and the need to put them to rest. Interesting, but nothing special.

Then I enter the second part.

What I encounter feels like receiving a steady stream of left hooks to the kidneys.

This section displays materials from the bombing: photographs, clothes, materials, and some body parts,

The last image I see before leaving are the remains of a tricycle. It belonged to a three-year-old boy. He was out on his trike when the bomb hit. Suffering deep burns, he died the next day.

It's too much. It's only a melted tricycle, but I see a photo of the little boy. I think of my little boys. How could someone do that? Did the pilots come to this museum? Did they see the remains of their actions?

I find the exit, step outside and sob. People watch. I don't care. I can't help it. It just comes.

Composed, I walk toward the Peace Memorial (aka A-Bomb Dome), a ruin from the bombing. It's a strange sensation to experience beauty and horror simultaneously. The walk alongside the Honkawa River is beautiful, reminding me of our own Rideau Canal back in Ottawa. Trees, paths and benches envelope the cold, hasty river. It would be a flawless image except for the menacing fixture to my right. The Dome is creepy. Reminds me of the Bates mansion from *Psycho*, except the horror here is real. I get a chill just looking at it. The Dome looms ominously over me like a giant. The roof is like a broken skull of metal. The bricks and mortar, scarred, disfigured and ruined, struggle to stand. Through the light of the windows I see the air moving. A slight wind creates a whistling sound. I peer through the cracked window frames and imagine the screams and pain. Chills bolt through my body. Nausea wallops my insides. Death right here, right now, still, always. The Dome, a living reminder of not just our inhumanity, but our mortality. Nothing. No one can deny or disguise that essential truth.

Sombre, touched, scared, I head back to the hotel. Memories of this past horror are quickly eclipsed by an assault of noise and light. You could walk through Hiroshima without any cognizance of its past. Looks like any other city. Neon icons of consumer culture enclose Hiroshima.

Before I reach the hotel I stop to watch a sumo match on the huge TV screen outside the American-style mall before heading inside to buy English books and underwear.

The next day, I hop on a bullet train to Kyoto.

Kyoto

Kyoto train station.

Maya Yonesho takes a train from Osaka to Kyoto.

She carries a notebook and a smile. Her hair falls beyond her shoulders, occasionally muting her eyes.

We sit in a mall coffee shop high above the newly constructed train station.

Clouds roll by the window.

Coffees are ordered.

I tell her that I'm lost.

"I can help you."

She opens up her notebook. Coloured slivers fly across the pages. Maya grabs my hand. "Let me show you." Her hand takes me into the notebook. She places me atop a light blue sliver.

Despite the velocity of the slivers, I feel immediate warmth. Coloured slivers fly and float around me, occasionally touching and merging before moving on. Chaotic connectedness. These brief, poignant connections and departures go on and on and on. Occasionally, the backgrounds change. For a few minutes we are in Norway, then Zagreb, Vienna, Tallinn. I'm startled when the space around us beings to fold in. Maya, flying on a nearby sliver, says it's OK. I just tried something different, folded each page into multiple pages. Soon it gets very cramped.

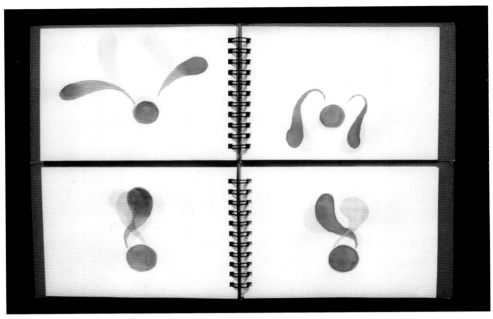

Figure 68.
Believe In It.

"I like notebooks very much", she shouts. "I don't want to lose original animated drawings, I did not want to use peg-bar or punching papers, I do not like the 'light box' because the light hits my eyes and I always need 'electricity' meaning I need a cable. If I draw on notebooks, I don't need to worry."

After a while, I grow bored. "Maya, it's all the same. Every page has the same style. I don't understand."

"Because I am always me", sings Maya. "You should fly with images, it's you. It is not to see but to ride on and fly with it. Then you can see something though your eyes."

All of this reminds me of something, but I can't remember what.

While ride through this white world of coloured rain, I ask Maya when she discovered this world.

"I found out if I use notebooks, I could use another frame in camera frame, means I can show 'several worlds' in one frame with several notebooks. Notebooks are also sort of diary, I

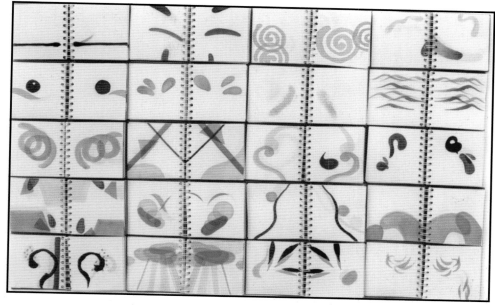

believe. Notebooks are symbol of diary, history, record, thought, ideas. … I like small things too…"

Figure 69.
Introspection

So many voices, different languages. "Introspection." "What goes around comes around." "You can do it." "You are fantastic."

I feel like I'm in a self-help nightmare. Images explode like soundwaves of the different voices. Everyone is so cheery and happy. The warm, gentle colours explode around me like giddy smiles. Soon, I stop hearing the languages of love and happiness … Maya translates them into pictures, universal imagery that need no words. Lines, circles and ribbons of colour flow in and out and around and under me. Kids' voices are heard. I see them as flying shapes. Everything is possible in Maya's world. Everyone is so god-damn happy in Maya's world.

Sudden darkness.

A door of light opens.

Images flow onto the pages of a journal. A solemn, creepy voice sings.

Figure 70. *Uks Uks*.

A new door opens. Each door is dressed as the cover of a journal. The design of the cover seems to dictate the tone of the flow of the contents. Church bells. Ribbons of colour fly toward me, growing faster by the second. Fast, light, slow, dark. On it goes. Finally, all the books come forward, their previously segregated images flow outward in and through the other books before returning to their domains.

I feel like I'm breathing the words of Heraclitus. Everything flows. Nothing is this same. Up and down are the same path. The straight and haggard are the same line. Everything is one. Something is familiar here. I'm sure I've been here before, once upon a time, a feeling so harmless, temporary like Achilles.

Suddenly, everything changes. The entire background of this world becomes real. Our ribbons of colour have become magic carpets. We travel through Vienna, Norway, Croatia and Taiwan. I feel like Santa Claus except we have no gifts.

Maya is frantically drawing on a notebook of Japanese rice paper. "JAPANESE BUDDHIST MONKS USE THIS PAPER

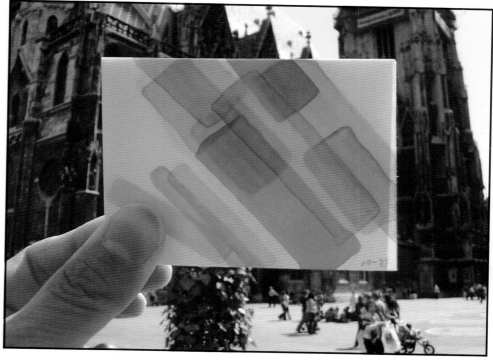

IN THEIR BIBLES. IT'S A THIN PAPER BUT QUITE WHITE AND A NICE SURFACE FOR MARKERS."

Figure 71. *Wiener Wuast*

She races to capture each site that we pass. We're living in a travel diary, experiencing her impressions and memory alongside the originals. Imagined and real unite. Past and present breathe together.

I feel a great sense of joy and freedom here, but it is transient. I know this will end, that I must leave.

Everything turns white. Maya takes my hand and we travel up through the whiteness. We reach the top and climb out of her notebook.

The coffees have arrived. Foams in the form of a bunny and a heart float atop our drinks.

We smile.

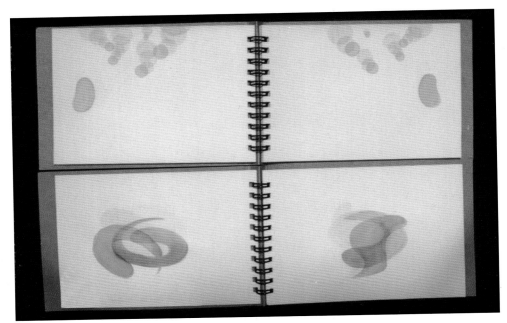

Figure 72. *Learn to Love..*

Figure 73. *Outside the Coffee Cup.*

Figure 74. *Puzzle of Autumn*

I feel good.

Maya suggests I visit the Kyoto University of Art and Design. She tells me to look for artists/animators **Keiichi Tanammi and Nobuhiro Aihara**.

So I do.

A visually odd couple.

Aihara is a poster child for hippies. Native-inspired paisley clothing. Long, jet black hair. Skirting between wild and raw black and white drawings and psychedelic Pollock, Aihara's work shouts madness, chaos, and harmony in manic bursts of spontaneity.

Tanammi comes across as a modest, mild-mannered accountant. His ubiquitous art, a sexy vibrant cross between psychedelia, pop art and goldfish (a constant figure in his work that comes from childhood memories), travels from painting, animation, installations and experimental film to a slew of merchandise (e.g. T-shirts, toys, shoes, watches, tattoos, handbags).

While Tanammi and Aihara have successful careers of their own, they're best known animations were made together. Collaborations are unique in animation. Occasionally, there are "jam" sessions like Marv Newland's *Pink Komkommer* or one-off collaborations like *Pro/Con* by Joanna Priestley and Joan Gratz, but nothing quite like Tanammi and Aihara.

They create the films together, each contributing half. Often they call their collaborations battles or correspondence. "Maybe I draw, then Aihara might delete some of mine. That's what we call battle. Other times we do correspondence. Maybe I send him a theme and he responds with his own pictures." It's a bit like the old call and response songs or jam sessions where musicians respond to each other.

"I thought it was interesting to have another artist and work together rather than using my own talent. We can stimulate each other and create new interesting work by fusing our styles."

How do you write about their work in a clear, linear manner?

You don't

So I won't.

Man washes faceless face. flowers flash in the background. naked woman. postcards. fish. submarine sound. doodle sketches morph into figures, continuing metamorphosis. animal/human

Figure 75. *Breath of Wind*.

figure united. explosions of colours. man plane. walking ear with
penis. body parts. tree face. man lumbering like a dream.
squiggles. no one is quite human. hands shake dance fly. fish in
room. stabbed sperm tadpoles, scattered fragments of identities.
nothing is whole. moments pass as they happen. like memories
unremembered. unsettling. shapes figures swirling clashing
spinning. recycled images. the slow motion flipping girl.
burning snail.

CALM. cherry blossoms.

Figure 76. *A Gaze in the Summer*.

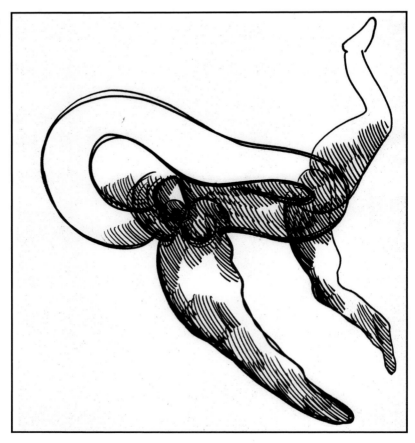

Search light. air raid siren. bombers. waves. rain. more penis ears. man walks, his shadow a woman. intimacy, stroking, touching, poking. exploding dick, cumming on flower. momentary violence. burning houses. flickering flood of colours. bombs explosions siren chaos. blown away. corpses.

Images flash by before you can process. fusion of daydream and memory. fragments of the senses. smells. tastes. sounds of past. things come together, fall apart. man and women bark at each other. strobe lights. layers of images flickering, violent, kinetic nightmare.

Hard to watch, comprehend. life in fast forward or rewind? need relief from this. imprints. traces of things that were.

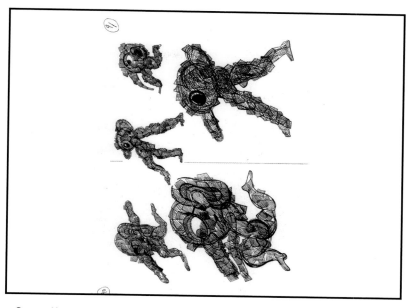

Figure 77.
*Memory of
Darkness, Dream
of Shadow*.

Sexuality. war. sex as war. war as sex. memories of grandfather
and goldfish. memories are dreams of what might have been.
fictions. nothing sure. nothing whole.

Whose dreams? Aihara? Tanammi?

who is who?

Figure 78.
*Memories
(Scene of
Childhood)*.

Figure 79. *A Gaze in the Summer*.

two is one. clash then fusion of memories, visions and fantasies.
an inconsistent cycle of chaos and harmony
then it ends.
until it begins again.
like life.
they do what they want when they want.

Kyoto is beautiful. The craziness of Tokyo erased by a calm,
traditional city that remains strongly rooted in its past. I decide
to be a tourist and wonder through the various landmarks: The

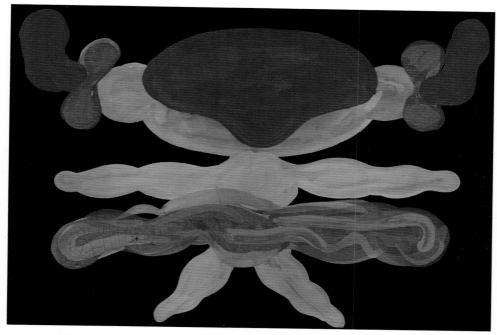

Figure 80. *Breath of Wind.*

Golden Temple, the Heian Shrine, Nijo Castle, the Ryoanji Temple with the rock garden.

I roam around the Higashiyama district. Lots of Geishas around here. Funny thing. I always thought that Geisha meant classy hooker or escort. Little did I know that they're actually traditional artists/entertainers. There ya go.

Walking along a canal, I read that I'm on the famous Philosopher's Path. The path got its name because one of Japan's most famous sages, Nishida Kitaro used to do his thinking here when he headed to the nearby university.

Exhausted, jet-lagged and feeling sick I grab a seat on a bench. I struggle to stay awake. Suddenly, I'm startled by three ghostly figures. They float above me. Their mouths don't move, but I hear them speak.

"You are forgetting us. We were here in the beginning."

"What are you talking about?"

109

They introduce themselves respectively as Kenzo Masaoka, Noburo Ofuji, Yasuji Murata.

"Ah ... OK ... I recognize your names. You guys were early Japanese animators."

"Yes. Why are you forgetting us?"

"Well, I'm not really. I was going to get around to it. Problem is that most of your works aren't readily available and even fewer exist with English subtitles. So, ya can't really blame me.

"Anyway ... since you're here, why don't we tell your stories now?"

Kenzou Masaoka is the first to speak.

Before he spoke, he did all the usual things: was born, studied art, learned about film by working on other people's projects, started his own company and made his own films.

Hanging with Masaoka is akin to being arm-locked with a woman (it's in the eye of the beholder 'natch, but I'm talking about the generic media/jock defined beauty) whose beauty is almost entirely superficial. It's not that he's vacuous, he's just a bit naive about the world. Sees only the beauty and good. Evil is temporary. It can be drowned like a spider in a puddle. A greedy grandmother can change her ways in an instant (how come we never find out why the old bitch cut her granddaughter's tongue out?).

Is this naive belief in our ability to POOF! PRESTO! change a sickness? Does Masaoka really believe that bad people can become good in a flash. He forces all the evil, bad, icky and yucky out of sight and mind, but it's still there, whether he wants to admit it or not.

We always give these old-timers a free pass. "Ah those were innocent times." Were they? A steady stream of big-ass wars and an economic collapse. Innocent times? Maybe things were just so bleak in reality that artists were desperate to find happiness

where they could – hence, the idealized worlds of early animation.

Figure 81. *Cherry Blossoms.*

Still, he's no idiot. The beauty of his vision is potent and genuine. He's a man of nature and sees beauty in simple things like flowers, ladybugs, and raindrops. Long grass caressed by the wind. Raindrops collapse to the ground with orchestrated, explosive beauty. Cherry blossoms and butterflies dance together, swooned by spring. Flowers on the hillside blooming crazy.

Masaoka catches the joy of the in-between moments. Plots exist solely to give him the freedom to celebrate the moments in our life that are taken for granted. His characters wander around the countryside, sniffing flowers, playing with animals, feeling the gentle brush of the falling cherry blossom pedals.

A mule catches sight of himself in a mirror. He's overcome with joy and amazement. It's as though the ass is seeing himself for the first time, really SEEING that, at this moment, he is alive and living.

111

And yeah, just so you feel comfortable, Masaoka's films are as good as anything being produced in the U.S. at that time. I like 'em better actually. Different worlds and perspectives. Crazy skating-in-shoes character movements, dizzying 360-degree camera shots, wavy landscapes that unsettle the characters.

His movie pals are a bit creepy at times, although maybe they just anticipate that wacky world of anime culture. There's this film featuring the recurring cat/boy character, Tora-Chan (a stock character is the first sign of an artist's demise unless you're Philip Roth). Are they cats or are they people? They have cat heads, but human faces and clothing. The characters remind me of the guy who dressed up in a real cat skin in Cornell Woolrich's *The Black Alibi*. Does Masaoka dream of a world where critters and people become one hybrid being? I ain't judging the man, just asking. One man's insanity is another guy's genius.

And hey, what's with that cat family structure. One mother, 4 kittens. Notice something odd about that? No Papa Cat. Was he hit by a wagon or burned in the golden temple (wait, that was later, I think). Seems pretty ballsy to present a single-parent family. And what's with the grandma who slices her grandaughter's tongue off? How does that happen? Why on Earth is the child living in a commune with other kids dressed in bird costumes (rivals of the cat people?).

Part moralist, part aesthete, Masaoka also likes a dose of nonsense. In one of his last films, *Tora-Chan*, (1947), a muscled sailor, a fish out of water, a black-faced monkey (oh so wrong!) and a ruffian gang of bandanna-clad octopuses chase and beat each other for no apparent reason.

In an earlier film, my personal fave, wingnut raccoon-dog creatures (actually they're called Tanuki) cause meaningless havoc in one film. Essentially, Tanukis are big-balled (seriously) agitators. They don't seem to have much purpose beyond being meddlesome pains in the ass. Imagine a politician or bureaucrat with big testicles and you get the idea.

I like this guy. He appreciates those overlooked moments of our lives, those times that we think are wasted. Masaoka sees them

as the highlights of the show. No moaning beret wearer though
– oh wait, he did wear a beret when he got older – Masaoka
clearly recognizes and appreciates the absurdity of existence. A
great man once said that accepting the absurdity of your
existence is the key to finding harmony during your life.

Next to speak is **Noburo Ofuji** (creator of the famous films,
Whale, 1927 and *Ghost Ship*, 1956). 1920s. No set identity. Heck,
wasn't even his real name. It was Shinshichiro Ofuji. Mother
died young. Raised by sister. Got into animation when he was a
teenager. Started making films in his late 20s. Dabbles in cut
out, cel, and silhouette. Was quite a pioneer. First-known
Japanese animator to use silhouette animation. Uses this special
Japanese coloured paper called chiyo (creator of the famous
films, Whale, 1927 and Ghost Ship, 1956) chiyogami in many
films. He made the first animation music videos in Japan, too.
Films like *Black Cat* (1929) featured two cats dancing in sync to
a live jazz record. His earliest film mixes live action and cut-out
to tell the story of an unusual relationship between a woman
and, well, umm, a cigarette. Phallic, anyone?

Ofuji was a talented guy, especially in the context of his time.
His films are enjoyable, playful, accessible with hints of poetry
and artistic ambitions.

The prominence of popular music recordings in Ofuji's films
brings to mind the cartoons of U.B. Iwerks and The Fleischer
Brothers. In fact, a number of Ofuji's films are little more than
music videos – good music videos. *Black Cat* is a silly film about
a dancing cat. *National Anthem Kimigayo* , (1931), is a somber
patriotic piece full of abstract, lyrical imagery. *Harvest Feast*,
(1930), offers a snippet of Japanese village life. *Song for Spring*,
(1931), is perhaps the most impressive of the vids. Using a single
colour (somewhere between lavender and cherry), Ofuji
celebrates the arrival of spring and love using a rich tapestry of
expressionistic designs.

The narrative films *Bear Dodger*, (1948), *Tengu Hunt*, (1934),
Chinkoroheibei and the Treasure Box (1936), are mild cautionary
tales tinged with absurdity and bouts of surrealism. Conflict,
greed and loyalty lie at the core of the three films.

Figure 82.
*Burglars of the
Baghdad Castle*.

In *Bear Dodger*, two travellers come together so they don't have to journey alone. However, conflict ensues when one of the travellers doesn't warn the other about an impending bear attack. The annoyed traveller tells the other guy to piss off and decides to go it alone. Apparently, it is better to go through hell alone than with someone else.

In *Treasure Box*, a bear/boy (so often it's hard to tell just what kind of animal is being portrayed) steals a treasure box from an undersea world. He attempts to flee to the surface, but is captured and turned into a dog.

Almost all of the early Japanese narrative animation films use either folk tales, fables or modern stories to create mild moralistic tales about the price deviants pay for their transgressions.

I want these films to touch me, but they don't. I can appreciate them. There is historical value I guess ... at least in the sense that Ofuji was there near the beginning helping to lay the carpet for future animators, giving them a sense of "Hey, I can do this too". And I'm sure animation historians (e.g. geeks) will ooze platitudes over the technical innovations and "adorable" designs of these early works and certainly there's some validity there, but they're no better or worse than any other films of the age.

To his credit, Ofuji didn't sit on his ass. He was out there working and challenging himself. He experimented with different styles, designs and tones. Artistic flourishes seep through occasionally, most notably in *Song for Spring* and *National Anthem*. Like Masaoka, Ofuji seems to understand the poetic and artistic possibilities of animation.

Finally, the third ghost, **Yasuji Murata** speaks. He seems a tad obsessive (aren't all animators though?) and maybe mildly moralistic, I think he might have been a pretty fun guy. His films, primarily aimed at children, are full of gags, adventure, crazy characters, and a dash of absurdity. His pace is often relentless. Little time is spent on setting up the story. The animation is fluid and well timed. The character designs are striking and unique.

Taro's Toy Train (1929) is the best example of Murata's unique ability to enter the mind of a child. Young Taro receives a toy train set from his Dad. While he sleeps, he dreams a train adventure. On board is an assortment of animal passengers. Taro is forced to resolve many conflicts. Finally, a fight breaks out between a monkey and bull. They smash through the train bringing Taro with them. They roll down a hill, hit the ground. Taro suddenly wakes up. Laughs at his dream and pulls out his trains.

Through Taro, Murata takes the viewer inside the vivid mind of a child, displaying the complexity and uniqueness and possibility of their imagination.

The bulk of Murata's films are morality tales – occasionally with conflicting messages. The *Monkey Sword Masamune* (1930) opens with a messenger frantically racing to deliver a message for his master. While he rests he hears a dog barking at monkeys in a tree. The monkeys hurt the dog. The dog's master tries to shoot the monkeys, but the messenger stops him. He does not believe in killing. Later though, the messenger slices a bull in half. Like a true human, the messenger has apparently forgotten his early stance against killing. What gives? Strange message for the kiddies.

Another rather bizarre message comes from *The Bat (1930)*. The film follows an all-out war between birds and beasts. Caught in the middle is a bat. He avoids capture by both sides by claiming to be either bird or beast. Finally, after the war ends, the beast and bird leaders demand that he clarify which side he is on. When he cannot, they banish him. Apparently, this is why bats hide during the day and appear only at night.

The message? If you don't conform, you're screwed. Emperor Hirohito must have eagerly approved of the film.

Why is the Sea Water Salty (1935) is part morality tale, part silly fable about, as the title says, how salt water began.

A poor man asks his older brother for food. Refused, the man walks away. After saving the life of an old man, he is given bean cakes and told to go to the forest and give them to dwarves in exchange for a stone mill. He does this and learns that when he turns the stone mill and makes a wish, it will come true. Soon, he becomes the richest guy in the village. His jealous brother steals the stone mill and flees to a deserted island. Along the way, he wishes for salt. Salt pours out and floods the boat. The boat sinks and the man is eaten by a shark. The stone mill falls to the bottom of the sea and keeps pumping out the salt.

Nice message about greed, but the punishment seems a tad harsh. Ah well. C'est la vie.

In *Sanko and the Octopus (1933)*, Sanko, a lazy no good husband prefers drinking, dancing and sleeping. While sleeping off a hangover, he dreams of chasing a treasure. The treasure is guarded by an octopus. A battle ensues along with a *It's A Mad, Mad World*-type chase. Animals, natives, octopus and Sanko all in hot pursuit of the treasure. Finally, the octopus retrieves the treasure box, opens it and his wife and children emerge. This is a true treasure.

Figure 83. *The Stolen Lump*.

Sanko awakens and apologizes to his wife for his bad behaviour. He vows to change.

Morality tales aside, *Sanko* shows Murata's always underling sense of humour. He uses the film to string together a series of physical gags (the octopus running on land is pretty damn funny.)

The Stolen Lump (1929) and *The Lark's Moving Day* (1933) follow the same righteous thread. The former suggests that no matter how miserable your existence might be, it can always be a hell of a lot worse. *The Lark's Moving Day*, a cynical tale about neighbours and community (or lack thereof) says that you can't rely on others to get the job done. You gotta do it yourself.

My fave of the bunch is *Over a Drink (1936)*. This time Murata forgoes his righteousness in favour of a straight comedy about a wandering hobo.

The hobo wanders the streets in search of food and drink. He picks up a paper describing investments where people can go and find a treasure aboard a sunken ship. Hobo laughs and wanders into a bar. He drinks, gets wasted and passes out.

Unconscious, the hobo dreams that he's underwater where he encounters some initially hostile samurais who later team with him to seek out a treasure on a nearby ship. They find the ship, but encounter a gaggle of ghost pirates. An absurd, violent surreal fight begins. Heads are sliced. Bodies cut in two. Touch of silent comedy influence. The hobo finds the treasure. As he attempts to flee the ship, the ghost pirates capture him. As they're about to kill him, he wakes up on the floor of the bar.

Awake in the bar, the owner gives him his bill. Broke he tells the keeper to find it on the sunken ship. Heh heh. Great line. No punishment. No morals. Just a loose and absurd farce about a wandering drunk.

Murata also made a string of yawners. *Our Baseball Match* (1931), *Sport's Day at Animal Village* (1932) and the *Momotaro* and *Norakuro* films are well-made adventure films that are really don't add up to much. Maybe the kiddies would get a laugh, but perhaps they'd snooze a bit, too.

Murata work is unique for its time. Combining gags and fables with a diversity of animation techniques, Murata's films stand up with any of American cartoons of the same era. In fact, they are arguably stronger films because they reach beyond being simple gag films.

The messages of Murata's films are often confusing. He seems to be both cynical and idealistic. All of the films show the beastly, hypocritical side of human nature, yet Murata seems to believe that bad people will get theirs in the end. It's a very innocent and naive view of the realities of the world – especially a world that would soon head into war. Occasionally, Murata swims into that dangerous polarized territory of simple categories of good and evil. On the other hand, in films like *Over a Drink* and *Monkey Sword,* he reveals a more insightful, informed awareness of the struggles and complexities of humanity.

American poet Walt Whitman said it best:

"Do I contradict myself?

Very well then I contradict myself,

(I am large, I contain multitudes.)"

And like that they're gone. Finally heard, I guess they've returned, content, to the highlands.

Highlands

Kamakura. West of Tokyo.

I'm walking through the middle of nowhere.

Lost in a forest of bamboo.

I look like I'm moving, but really just standing still.

I ain't in a hurry to leave.

Everything is gonna be alright.

That's what they keep telling me

I close my eyes and wonder.

A friend appears. **Koji Yamamura**.

He leads me out of the forest.

We walk down a path.

"In the spring", Koji tells me, "the cherry trees blossom and the path explodes with beautiful colours".

Cherry blossoms make me think of Koji's film *Atama Yama*, (2002). It was his first major success, won him an Oscar nomination. It's about this stingy asshole who hoards everything in his dump of a house. When he eats cherries he finds on the ground a cherry tree sprouts from his head. Soon

Figure 84. *Forest of Bamboo.*

people come to picnic and socialize around the tree on his head. Angry with their noise and waste, he shakes them off his head and eventually ends up killing himself.

Atama Yama was a surprising film. Koji's previous works were generally gentle, set in the world of children. Koji's films celebrated the magnificence of the mundane, the beauty of the moment. *Atama Yama* was so much darker, giving us a despicable anti-social character who thinks of no one but himself, who derives no pleasure from life.

The man has forgotten life.

Have I forgotten life? Barry's death swallows me, drowning me in a sea of grief and terror. Here. Gone. Like that. Ashes. What was the point of it all? What IS the point of it all? What of my children? Why did I have kids? Giving them breath to die?

I hear these existential thoughts and cringe. Everyone goes through this "what's the point" crap. I wanna go back to Koji's world, his earlier films. They remind me of my childhood and

Figure 85. *Atama Yama*.

my children's. That overwhelming sense of the moment. There is no past or future in their world. In a fever of scattered senses they embrace, life, smile and cry the moment. It's in these small moments that we find the essence of our lives. To live in the moment is to savour each morsel. No matter how seemingly insignificant, the crumbs make the man.

Koji's films seek the essence of life within these small, and too often overlooked, moments. In this world, life is sacred. Every ounce is consumed and enjoyed. Life is pleasure. Pleasure comes from those individual moments. The characters Karo and Pyrobupt are the anti-Vladimir and Estragon from *Waiting for Godot*. They await no one. They embrace the moment. In *A House*, (1993), they build a house together before winter approaches. In *Imagination*, (1993), they use their imagination to forget about a rainy day. Friendship. Collaboration. Communication. Imagination. Satisfaction. That's it. That's all. Life shared. Life loved.

In *Bavel's Book* (1996) and *Kid's Castle* (1995), the excitement, power and realism of the objects only exist because of the tenacity of imagination within each child. Without the

Figure 86.
Sandwiches.

children's ability to let go and share themselves with their book or toy, they remain objects, fragments of a dead tree littered with indecipherable ink stains.

In the world of the child, the mundane is as significant as the spiritual. Children see the greatness in little things. They don't worry about the end, or the deed, existing only for the process. The completing not the completion.

Koji unearths the forgotten spaces, the cracks, gaps, and out-of-frame moments that embody the essence of adult and child. The unframed memories breathed as the irrevocable instant of a child.

In *Your Choice* (1999), moments are defined by choices we make. Will it rain or shine? Do I need an umbrella? Shall I visit the barber or dentist? Choices involve the untangling of emotions and reason. Choices involve communication with experience, the experience of our past or the wisdom of those who've gone before us.

Figure 87. *Your Choice*.

To choose does not necessarily mean to be free. Raoul, the central character, has choices forced upon him. If he had chosen to take care of his hair and teeth, he would not be making these painful choices. In the end Raoul avoids making a decision. His pain becomes so bad he runs to the dentist. The waiting room is full. The only choice is the barber. What Raoul doesn't yet understand is that if we avoid choices, they will be made regardless.

Sometimes, we make bad choices. Sometimes, we can go too far and turn a moment into a womb, a shelter from those around us. In *Atama Yama*, the stingy man lives not as an echo, but as a shadow. He is surrounded by garbage, a rubbishy ramification that staves off the threshold of despair. He wastes nothing. He shares nothing. He enjoys nothing. Cherries are shoved into his mouth untasted. When he chooses to let a tree grow on his head, it becomes an attraction for Tokyo workers. They take and take. He can't handle it and pulls the tree out. All that remains is a hole. People come to fish instead. The man flees in horror and finally kills himself by jumping into the hole in his head. Ecological warning aside, a man who embraces only himself, lives and dies alone.

125

Figure 88. *Atama Yama..*

Figure 89. *Franz Kafka's Country Doctor*.

The Old Crocodile, (2006), features another selfish character. His choices are based solely on self-preservation. He will destroy family and friends in order to survive. In the end he is rewarded and given all he can eat when he becomes a false idol. However, on deeper more meaningful level he has sacrificed everything that is important in life (family and friendship) for false and superficial worship.

Figure 90. *Franz Kafka's Country Doctor.*

In Koji's masterpiece, *Franz Kafka's a Country Doctor,* (2007), we encounter an insane, burned-out and cynical doctor (Koji conveys his madness and anxiety through some amazing animation that has the man squirming, shaking, and stretching). On a cold winter night, he makes a choice to see a sick child. A man provides him with horses. The doctor leaves even though he knows that his servant will be raped by the man.

As the doctor examines the dying boy, voices clash in his head. He has lost faith in the world and in himself: "I myself wish I could die ... I have no desire to remake the world".

The boy asks the doctor if he can save him.

"What do you want of me?" asks the doctor. "What would you have me do?"

Who is sicker? Who is really in need of saving?

The ailing boy can see the doctor's madness. "I have no faith in you", he tells the doctor.

The doctor finally flees from the house. Stark naked, he rides home. He arrives frozen, shaken, alone.

Existence has overwhelmed him. No longer busy being born, the old doctor is too busy dying.

"The old doctor", Koji says, "is thrown naked to the world of uneasiness. He is the metaphor which symbolizes all human beings. We were all thrown into this world. We cried a lot when we were born."

"Koji, do you believe in free will?"

"I don't have an answer to this question yet, but I never believe in determinism so maybe I stand for free will. The thought of fatalism is a little bit near my actual feeling. I don't believe in the thought that time has a strict and linear order. I even doubt our existence itself so sometime I think free will is an illusion, too. The thought of free will won't exist if there are no humans in the world. I prefer such kind of thought."

"'You're Born, you die', I wrote in another space. In between, you try and do a bit of this and a bit of that while mingled together with a bunch of other people who were born at the same time and who are also trying to do a bit of this and a bit of that. We're all strung together in a single book trying to create our own verse before the page turns. To leave and live a unique ineradicable stain of memories and moments that bleed through the pages is not the best we can hope for, to try is. "

We enter the tea room through a small door. As we pass through the door we bow. The room is bare void of paint, colours, objects. Koji leads me to a bench. We sit. Soon a woman enters. Kneeling behind a small table she carefully scoops green tea powder from a container into a ceramic tea bowl. Hot water

follows the tea powder into the bowl. Finally she grabs a tea whisk and whips the water and powder together.

Figure 91. *A Drink in Silence.*

The tea is brought to us. Koji explains what we must do next. I am to gently lift the tea bowl with my right hand and place it onto the palm of my left hand. I then rotate the bowl clockwise twice so that the right side of the bowl is at the front.

We drink in silence.

Calmness overwhelms me. The warmth of the tea swallows me whole.

I close my eyes and feel the wrongness of life fade with each sip.

It's almost like I don't exist.

Sobs suddenly explode from within.

129

No one moves.

Tears, pain, howls are sent forth.

Time passes by.

Stillness returns.

Worn down by weeping.

Outside, Koji looks at me and says "I think you're ready to return home".

As we part, I think I hear him say, "treasure every meeting, for it will never recur".

Early morning.

Haven't slept a wink.

Heading to the airport.

Time to go home.

Party time is over.

A friend has gone.

I got nothing more to say.

A sumo wrestler stands in front of me.

Won't let me pass.

Wears a black mawashi

Pale face.

Looks deathly.

Seems like I gotta fight this rikishi ("strong man")

How can I win against something so inevitable?

He invites me into the dohyo.

I oblige. Seems I have no choice.

I know nada about sumo.

Saw a match in Tokyo.

We take our places and assume the Shikiri (essentially, like the posture of a offensive lineman in football).

He brings his hands up and puts them on his knees.

Lifts legs one at a time and stomps.

I follow suit, feelings like an idiot.

We resume the Shikiri.

Before I'm ready, he lunches forward, head down.

I swiftly move out of the way.

He turns and starts to hit me with open hands.

Hurts like hell. I keep shuffling to avoid the full impact of his weight.

Sweat falls. I reach for his fat sides, but he pushes me aside.

Off balance, he sees a chance and grabs my throat.

He pushes me back. I try to resist, but feet slide along the sand.

I feel the edge of the ring with my feet.

I struggle to breathe.

Desperate, I use all the power I have left and kick him in the balls.

As he falls in pain I rush at him, head first and send him flying out of the ring.

Flat on his ass, he grabs his balls.

He's pissed off and shouts at me, "You cheated".

"Hey man you gotta do what you gotta do to survive."

He shrugs. "We'll meet again. It's inevitable that I will one day win."

I say nothing. I know he's right.

Walking on, I see that the sun is beginning to shine.

It's not like the way the sun used to be.

My eyes feel new.

Everything looks so far away.

There's gotta be a way to get there.

I'll figure it out sometime.

But at least I know that my mind is already there.

And that's OK for now.

Select Filmography

Nobuhiru Aihara
Poisonous Snake, 1971
Aisanka, 1973
Cloud Thread, 1976
Water Wheel, 1980
Shadow, 1987
Mask, 1991
Air Power, 1994
Yellow Fish, 1998
Memory of Red, 2004

Nobuhiro Aihara/Keiichi Tanammi
Scrap Diary, 2002
Fetish, 2003
Landscape, 2004
10 Nights' Dreams, 2004

Taku Furukawa
Oxed-Man 1968
New York Trip, 1970
Head Spoon, 1972
Nice To See You, 1975
Beautiful Planet, 1974
Phenakistiscope, 1975
Coffee Break, 1977
Motion Lumine, 1978
Comics, 1979
Speed, 1980
Sleepy, 1980
Portrait, 1983
The Bird, 1985
Mac The Movie, 1985
Calligraphiti, 1982

Play Jazz, 1987
Direct Animation, 1987
TarZAN, 1990
From Heart to Heart, 1992
Tokyo Story, 1999

Kunio Kato
The Apple Incident, 2001
Fantasy, 2003
The Diary of Tortov Roddle, 2003
The House of Small Cubes, 2008

Kihachiro Kawamoto
The Breaking of Branches Is Forbidden, 1968
An Anthropo-Cynical Farce, 1970
The Demon, 1972
The Trip, 1973
A Poet's Life, 1974
Dojoji Temple, 1976
House of Flames, 1979
The Book of the Dead, 2005

Keita Kurosaka
Sea Roar, 1988
The Worm Story, 1989
Personal City, 1990
Haruko Adventure, 1991
Box Age, 1992
Head, 1994
Flying Daddy, 1997
Dragon, 1999
Agitated Screams of Maggots, 2006

Renzo Kinoshita
What on Earth is He?, 1971
Made in Japan, 1972
Japonese, 1977
Picadon, 1978
Geba Geba Showtime, 1986
Frame of Mind, 1990
The Last Air Raid Kumagaya, 1993

The Little Journey, 1994
Made in Okinawa, 2004

Yoji Kuri

Fashion, 1960
Stamp Fantasia, 1961
Two Pikes, 1961
Human Zoo, 1962
Love, 1963
Man and a Woman and a Dog, 1963
The Discovery of Zero, 1963
Miracle, 1963
AOS, 1964
The Chair, 1964
The Button, 1964
The Man Next Door, 1965
A Small Sound, 1966
The Room, 1967
What Are You Thinking?, 1967
Au Fou!, 1968
Tragedy on the G Line, 1969
The Midnight Parasites, 1972
POP, 1974
MANGA, 1977

Kenzo Masaoka

A Dance Song with a Kettle, 1934
Benkei vs Ushiwaka, 1939
The Spider and The Tulip, 1943
Cherry Blossom, 1947
Tora-Chan, an Orphan Kitty, 1947
Tora-Chan's Wedding, 1948
Tora-Chan's Ship Sweeper, 1950

Mirai Mizue

Fantastic Cell, 2003
Minamo, 2003
Trip-Trap, 2005
Adamski, 2008
Lost Utopia, 2008
Devour Dinner, 2008
Jam, 2009

Yasuji Murata
Animal Olympics, 1928
The Stolen Lump, 1929
Taro's Train, 1929
The Monkey Masamune, 1930
Our Baseball Match, 1931
Momotaro's Sky Adventure, 1931
Momotaro's Underwater Adventure, 1932
Sports Day at Animal Village, 1932
The Lark's Moving Day, 1933
Private 2nd Class Norakuro, 1933
Corporal Norakuro, 1934
Why is the Sea Water Salty, 1935
Over a Drink, 1936

Noburo Ofuji
Whale, 1927
The Black Cat, 1929
Harvest Festival, 1930
National Anthem Kimigayo, 1931
Spring Song, 1931
Tengu Hunt, 1934
Chinkoroheibei and the Treasure Box, 1936
The Bear Dodger, 1948
Ghost Ship, 1956

Tadanari Okamoto
A Wonderful Medicine, 1965
Welcome, Alien, 1966
Operation Woodpecker, 1966
Back When Grampa was a Pirate, 1968
Ten Little Indians, 1968
Home My Home, 1970
The Flower and the Mole, 1970
Chikotan, 1971
Lonely Valley, 1971
December Song, 1971
The Monkey and the Crab, 1972
The Tree of Mochimochi, 1972
Praise Be to Small Ills, 1973
The Traveling Companion, 1973
Five Small Stories, 1974
The Water Seed, 1975

Deep Sea Fish, 1975
The Prince with the Big Belly, 1975
The Phone Booth, 1975
Symphonic Variations, 1976
Who's That?, 1976
The Strong Bridge, 1976
From Cherry Blossom with Love, 1976
Towards the Rainbow, 1977
Letter on a Snowy Day, 1978
Panache the Squirrel, 1978
Beautiful Name, 1979
The Soba Flower of Mt. Oni, 1979
Forgotten Doll, 1980
Shhh!, 1980
Grampa Frypan, 1981
White Elephant, 1981
The Magic Ballad, 1982
Human Evolution, 1982
The Surly Donkey, 1983
Metropolitan Museum, 1984
Coro's on the Roof, 1986
The Restaurant of Many Orders, 1991

Kei Oyama
Nami, 2000
Usual Sunday, 2003
The Thaw, 2004
Consultation Room, 2005
Anizo, 2006
Yuki-Chan, 2006
Hand Soap, 2008

Keeichi Tanaami
Easy Friday, 1975
4 Eyes, 1975
Another Rainbow-Colored City, 1979
Yoshikei, 1979
Memory of Darkness, Dream of Shadow, 2000
Breath of Wind (2001, w/Nobuhiro Aihara)
Summer Gaze – 1942, 2002
Memories, 2002
Goldfish Fetish, 2002
Running Man (2002 w/Nobuhiro Aihara)

Why?, 2002
Puzzle of Autumn, 2003

Osamu Tezuka
Tales of the Street Corner, 1962
Male, 1962
Memory, 1964
Mermaid, 1964
The Drop, 1965
Pictures at an Exhibition, 1965
The Genesis, 1968
Jumping, 1984
Broken Down Film, 1985
Push, 1987
Muramasa, 1987
Legend of the Forest, 1987
Self Portrait, 1988

Naoyuki Tsuji
Wake Up, 1992
For Almost Forgotten Stories, 1994
The Rule of Dreams, 1995
A Feather Stare at the Dark, 2003
Trilogy About Clouds, 2005
Children of the Shadows, 2006
The Place Where We Were, 2008

Koji Yamamura
Aquatic, 1988
Perspektive Box, 1989
The Elevator, 1991
Imagination, 1993
The Sandwiches, 1993
A House, 1993
Kid's Castle, 1995
Kipling Jr., 1995
Pacusi, 1996
Your Choice, 1999
Mt. Head, 2002
The Old Crocodile, 2006
Franz Kafka's A Country Doctor, 2007
A Child's Metaphysics, 2007

Maya Yonesho
Don't You Wish You Were Here?, 1997
Believe In It, 1998
Introspection, 1998
Learn to Leave, 1999
Countdown, 2002
Winter Days Segment, 2002
Uks Uks, 2003
Wiener Wuast, 2006
Daumenreise series:
Poland, Taiwan, Croatia, Norway, Kyoto, Israel, 2007–2008

Atsushi Wada
Dancer of Vernacular, 2004
Day of Nose, 2005
Manipulated Man, 2006
Well, That's Glasses, 2007

Acknowledgements

If not for the support of Toshi Yonehara, of the Japan Embassy in Ottawa, who encouraged me to apply for a Japan Foundation visitor's grant, this book would not exist.

Oddly enough, I was anything but lost during my two-week trip to Japan in January 2007. Throughout the trip I was accompanied by animators, translators and escorts. Thanks to them all for making an amazing trip even more rewarding.

Thanks to Eriko Hoshino, Jerrett Zaroski, Jennifer Noseworthy, Azarin Sohrabkhani, Theodore Ushev, Tom McSorley, Maral Mohammadian, Peter Jupp, Andrea Stokes, Michael Fukushima, and Kelly, Betty, Jarvis and Harry Neall.

Big thanks to David Ehrlich for his advice and suggestions and John Libbey for his continual support of my work and independent animation in general.

Big, big thanks to Pauline Colwin for taking time out of her mind to edit this book.

I also want to acknowledge an array of sources that helped me gain a grasp of Japanese culture and society: David Benjamin's *The Joy of Sumo,* Ben Ettinger's amazing Anipages website, *The Japanese Mind* by Roger Davies and Osamu Ikeno, and Nobuo Mochizuki's brief outline of early Japanese animation. And, of course, I owe Bob Dylan and Big Bird for their inspiration.

I also want to thank every animator in this book for making time for me. Their generosity when I visited them and later hounded them with emails will not be forgotten.

I simply cannot give enough thanks to my friends Sayoko Kinoshita and Koji Yamamura. Their support, advice and help went beyond the call of duty.

Finally, I thank Nobuaki Doi, who helped me in so many ways. He arranged for photos, translated interview questions, corrected my Japanese words and their meanings. He also helped flesh out and write the Japanese animation history section. Without his friendship and help, I could not have written this book.